Math Anxiety

HOW TO BEAT
TEST ANXIETY
AND
SCORE HIGHER
ON YOUR EXAMS

by

Dr. James H. Divine
David W. Kylen

Barron's Educational Series, Inc.
New York • London • Toronto • Sydney

All inquiries should be addressed to:
Barron's Educational Series, Inc.
250 Wireless Boulevard
Hauppauge, New York 11788

Library of Congress Catalog Card No. 79-14251

Paper Edition
International Standard Book No. 0-8120-2091-X

Library of Congress Cataloging in Publication Data
Divine, James H
   How to beat test anxiety and score higher on your
exams.
   1. Examinations. 2. Test anxiety. 3. Study, Method of. I.
Kylen, David W., joint author.
   II. Title.
LB3051.D57   371.2'6   79-14251
ISBN 0-8120-2091-X

II   PRINTED IN THE UNITED STATES OF AMERICA

890   550   987654.

CONTENTS

Introduction

Introduction

Today is the day for an important examination. The scene is familiar. An individual arrives to take a test after several days of annoying worry about how well he or she will do compared to others.

The other people are arriving, too. Their presence is not very reassuring. Some are making small talk and nervous little witticisms. Others appear confident and eager. (It's difficult to tell whether or not this is just for appearances.) There seems to be a general tension in the air.

Everyone is seated and briefed, military style. They have officially become "test takers." The persons administering the test seem cold and uncaring. This is going to be a long day. "Did anyone bring aspirin?"

For most people examinations are threatening and give rise to anxiety. If it is a very important test, the anxiety generated can be brain numbing. The thought that your entire future could be affected by your performance can be downright paralyzing. If only there were some other way than taking tests.

Let's be realistic. You must take tests if you want to achieve your goals. This is a test-oriented society. It is futile to discuss whether it should be this way or not. The fact remains: You must take tests!

So let's talk instead about some things which have a bearing on how well you will do (assuming that you are motivated to do well). There are three basic factors.

First, and no doubt foremost, is the amount of knowledge you have stored away in your brain—the *knowledge factor*. There are years of experiences, facts, and judgments crammed into that softball-sized computer of yours. Tests are designed to tap some of that information.

Second, your skills at taking tests will help determine how well you will do. Your experiences and tactics in test taking and your familiarity with the forms and logic of tests are important. This is the *test-taking skills factor*.

Third, the amount of anxiety which you bring along with you to the exam will also affect your performance—the *test anxiety factor*.

Test takers are all too well aware of the knowledge factor. Some people have actually tried to cram for a college entrance exam. Keep in mind that such tests are designed to measure knowledge acquired over long periods of time. Cramming, more often than not, confuses the test taker and gives rise to more anxious feelings.

No one book can resolve the knowledge problem. Of course knowledge is important, but our observations show that most test takers fail to give thoughtful consideration to the second and third factors. Studies by psychologists and educators show that test-taking skills and test anxiety are very important determinants of success. In addition, test takers can actually improve their scores significantly by giving even a small amount of the right kind of attention to these factors before taking tests.

Complete preparation is the key to successful test taking. It is a *whole person* taking the exam, a complex individual with strong emotional feelings who must be under control when he or she is trying to use clear judgment during a test.

In short, knowledge alone is not enough on important exams. Many people believe that if you have a good command of the subject to be tested, then test-taking skills and test anxiety will not be problems. We now know that this is not true. No matter what degree of knowledge you may possess, deficiencies in handling the test-taking skills and the test anxiety factors could interfere with your test performance. You could be an authority on a given topic and yet not be able to show it on a test because you feel threatened, anxious, or have poor test-taking skills. One of the authors saw a student walk out of his doctoral exams without answering any of the test questions. He wrote "I don't know" in his exam book and walked out. These were the final exams to be taken before receiving his degree. Did he lack knowledge of his field? Certainly not or he would not have gotten that far in the doctoral program. What happened? He was literally overcome with test anxiety. A master's degree candidate had a similar experience, but she was more fortunate than the preceding fellow. Her committee of professors was more sympathetic than his. They told her she could retake the exam, but first she must go through a counseling program that would help her reduce her test anxiety.

Countless people—students and employees—approach exams without any thought given to either the skills needed or the anxiety involved in taking tests. It is as if a plumber would arrive at the job full of knowledge of plumbing but without any tools.

There is nothing in this book that will give you a higher score than you really deserve. This book is meant to help you achieve the score you truly merit.

We will show you how to: (1) improve your test-taking skills, thereby making you more test-wise; and (2) control and reduce your test anxiety and build self-confidence, allowing you to score higher.

ACKNOWLEDGMENTS

We gratefully acknowledge the critical suggestions of our friend James Fisher. We thank Barbara Sherman for her expedient typing of the manuscript. We also would like to thank Lavonne Mueller for her astute comments and helpful suggestions.

PART I

THE
TEST ANXIETY
FACTOR

CHAPTER 1

Your Test Anxiety

Did you ever observe the behavior of people who were taking a test? Some of them squirm and fidget in their seats. Others unknowingly tap their fingers or tug on their hair or ears. Some jiggle their knees up and down. Others cough and sniffle. Still others nervously respond to irrelevant room noises. A small number stare vacantly at the ceiling wasting time. Some sit in a tense, almost frozen posture, moving only their eyes and hands. No one seems relaxed.

These physical characteristics are called body language and tell us something is happening inside a person, something which interferes with performance in taking tests. It is called test anxiety. Test anxiety is a special, intense kind of nervousness that arises from the total test situation. It keeps the test taker from scoring as well as he might. Authorities in the field report that most people taking tests have test anxiety. Do you? The purpose of this chapter is to help you understand and analyze your apprehensiveness of tests.

Is some test anxiety good for you? A few educators believe a small amount of anxiety serves to spark the thought processes, to alert the person, or to quicken mental responses. This is a misunderstanding of test anxiety. Researchers find that anxiety, like alcohol, 3 acts as a depressant, not a stimulant. Test anxiety is a negative nervous reaction which does more harm than good. The proper, beneficial motivation for all forms of evaluation is positive excitement, not fear (the basis of test anxiety). Positive excitement is enjoyable anticipation of accomplishment. It involves positive reactions without self-doubt. Beneficial motivation is possible only after the removal of test anxiety.

If you are bothered by some or all of the following characteristics, you may be suffering from this problem:

1. You feel that tests are more of a threat than a challenge.
2. You have a lot of worrisome or negative thoughts about what might happen if you do poorly.
3. You have physical reactions (such as butterflies in the stomach, sweaty palms, altered heart or breathing rate) when you are about to take a test.
4. You have trouble keeping your mind on the test items or remembering ideas you learned recently.
5. You worry about other people scoring higher than you on the test.
6. Your worries about tests have not decreased as you have matured.

We have found that most people experience some or all of the preceding at some time when taking tests. We think test takers can overcome their fear of tests. So do not think yourself hopeless if you, too, said yes to some or all of the above.

When you are being evaluated in a life situation and the outcome is important to you, your reaction consists of two basic responses: (1) you attempt to perform the required task as well as possible, and (2) you react emotionally to being evaluated. When you audition or interview for a job you want, you try to demonstrate your skill and competence. But you also react emotionally. In athletic competition, you apply your knowledge and skill, and you react emotionally. When the evaluation you go through has important consequences for you, your emotional response more often than not is of the sort that interferes with your performance. On the other hand, the more dispassionate your reaction the better the performance.

One of the authors was part of a team investigating candidates for a job. An applicant, well qualified on paper, was given a low evaluation because of his inability to cope with his emotional reaction to being interviewed. He was so nervous and shaky he made the whole committee nervous. His emotional stability was questioned and he was not selected. However, he was known by acquaintances to be emotionally stable. The job was given to someone who was equally qualified but who had more control over his emotions while being interviewed.

Athletes know that when competitors in a sport are nearly equal in ability, those who "keep cool" emotionally have the advantage. Sometimes an athlete, knowing this, will try to psych out the opponent, forcing an error that otherwise would not be committed. It is often this emotional aspect that counts in competition.

A person's anxiety reactions usually produce negative results. Emotions clutter up logical thought processes. Negativism and worry scatter and disrupt the attention process. Test anxiety produces mental interferences that allow one neither to think clearly nor to concentrate on the test items. The whole situation becomes intimidating. One tends to become more concerned with protecting basic feelings of adequacy than with coping directly with the situation. In such a defensive orientation, one is less able to face the situation objectively. Mental perception narrows. One becomes less flexible in thinking and less inventive. Emotional reaction also can mobilize the body for action when no appropriate action is called for. One becomes "hyper." This can be a further burden because it acts to reinforce the anxiety. Research indicates that these interferences get worse the more difficult the test.

How do we develop test anxiety responses? Psychologists and educators conclude that test anxiety is something that we *learn*. We have been conditioned or programmed to become nervous at the thought of taking an exam. It is a learned reaction pattern forced upon us from our environment. But we must realize that neither we nor others are to blame. The problem is born of circumstances. This does not, however, excuse us from dealing with these anxieties in an intelligent way.

Test anxiety responses form a kind of trap that we fall into at an early age and from which we may never escape unless we change some of our thinking patterns and habits. Consider the following experiences of children:

Billy (age 7) notices that his mother gets concerned when he mentions he will have a test in school tomorrow.

Jill (age 6) sees that the teacher favors those students who can answer questions correctly. Jill is not one of them.

Jackie (age 8) observes that his mother has on several occasions told, with a frowning face, about how Dad couldn't get a better job because he couldn't pass certain tests.

Debby (age 6) feels hurt because she overhears her father tell her mother that Debby's school entrance tests indicate that she is going to have "problems."

These examples (and many others you may recall from your own experience) indicate the kind of soil in which test anxiety can begin to grow. The harvest contains unreasonable self-expectations, fears of failure and negative attitudes toward tests.

As students progress through their schooling, test anxiety may become more of a problem. In an extreme example, a high school senior with a B grade average told the authors that she had changed her plans to enter college when she was told she must take a college entrance exam. It was too frightening. She said she could barely handle the anxiety encountered with her regular classroom tests!

People do not ordinarily have to be told that they are nervous when they are about to take an important exam. They feel it. But most people are not conscious of all the symptoms or expressions of their anxiety and the harm done by it. Chances are you have not taken the time to pinpoint your own unique sources and manifestations of test-induced fear.

This analysis of test anxiety is often something people consciously avoid as they would some unpleasant odor. Consequently, neither the problem nor the solution is faced until it is fully and accurately perceived. This is your first step: take an honest look inward to spot and to define the problems.

To help you pinpoint your problems, we have prepared a list of statements: your Test Anxiety Inventory. You are to read each one and see if it reflects your experience in test taking.

If it does, place a check mark on the line next to the number of the statement. Check as many as seem fitting. Check an item if you can possibly see yourself in such a situation or thinking such thoughts. Be totally honest with yourself. When you answer, do not contemplate long. Answer by going with your first inclination. You might wish to go back after you finish for further consideration of certain responses. If you answer quickly, however, your answer may come from a true feeling which you might rationalize away if you were to reflect on your answer too long. If you have difficulty deciding, we recommend that you place a check mark next to the statement anyway, because it may indicate an underlying or related concern. After you finish we will show you what to do with your self-analysis list.

Your Test Anxiety Inventory

_____ 1. I wish there were some way to succeed without taking tests.

_____ 2. Getting a good score on one test does not seem to increase my confidence on other tests.

_____ 3. People (family, friends, etc.) are counting on me to do well.

_____ 4. During a test I sometimes find myself having trains of thought that have nothing to do with the test.

_____ 5. I do not enjoy eating before or after an important test.

_____ 6. I have always dreaded courses in which the teacher has the habit of giving "pop" quizzes.

_____ 7. It seems to me that test sessions should not be made the formal, tense situations they are.

_____ 8. People who do well on tests generally end up in better positions in life.

_____ 9. Before or during an important exam, I find myself thinking of how much brighter some of the other test takers are than I am.

_____ 10. Even though I don't always think about it, I am concerned about how others will view me if I do poorly.

_____ 11. Worrying about how well I will do interferes with my preparation and performance on tests.

_____ 12. Having to face an important test disturbs my sleep.

_____ 13. I cannot stand to have people walking around watching me while I take a test.

_____ 14. If exams could be done away with, I think I would actually learn more from my courses.

_____ 15. Knowing that my future depends in part on doing well on tests upsets me.

_____ 16. I know I could outscore most people if I could just "get myself together."

_____ 17. People will question my ability if I do poorly.

_____ 18. I never seem to be fully prepared to take tests.

_____ 19. I cannot relax physically before a test.

_____ 20. I mentally freeze up on important tests.

_____ 21. Room noises (those coming from lights, heating/cooling systems, other test takers, etc.) bother me.

_____ 22. I have a hollow, uneasy feeling before taking a test.

_____ 23. Tests make me wonder if I will ever reach my goals.

_____ 24. Tests do not really show how much a person knows.

_____ 25. If I score low, I am not going to tell anyone exactly what my score was.

_____ 26. I often feel the need to cram before a test.

_____ 27. My stomach becomes upset before important tests.

_____ 28. I seem to defeat myself (think negative thoughts) sometimes while working on an important test.

_____ 29. I start feeling very anxious or uneasy just before getting test results.

_____ 30. I wish I could get into a vocation that

does not require tests for entrance.

_____ 31. If I do not do well on this test, I guess it will mean I am not as smart as I thought I was.

_____ 32. If my score is low, my parents will be very disappointed.

_____ 33. My anxiety about tests makes me want to avoid preparing fully, and this just makes me more anxious.

_____ 34. I often find my fingers tapping or my legs jiggling while taking a test.

_____ 35. After taking a test, I often feel I could have done better than I actually did.

_____ 36. When taking a test, my emotional feelings interfere with my concentration.

_____ 37. The harder I work on some test items, the more confused I get.

_____ 38. Aside from what others may think of me, I am concerned about my own opinion of myself if I do poorly.

_____ 39. My muscles tense up in certain areas of my body when I take a test.

_____ 40. I do not feel confident and mentally relaxed before a test.

_____ 41. My friends will be disappointed in me if my score is low.

_____ 42. One of my problems is in not knowing exactly when I am prepared for a test.

_____ 43. I often feel physically panicky when I have to take a really important test.

_____ 44. I wish test evaluators could recognize that some individuals are more nervous than others in taking tests, and that this fact could be taken into account when test results are evaluated.

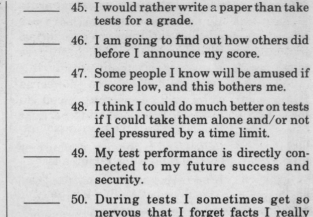

_____ 45. I would rather write a paper than take tests for a grade.

_____ 46. I am going to find out how others did before I announce my score.

_____ 47. Some people I know will be amused if I score low, and this bothers me.

_____ 48. I think I could do much better on tests if I could take them alone and/or not feel pressured by a time limit.

_____ 49. My test performance is directly connected to my future success and security.

_____ 50. During tests I sometimes get so nervous that I forget facts I really know.

Now that you have gone through the checklist and have indicated items with which you can identify, let us continue with the analysis of your test anxiety. The checklist was composed of items from two broad categories: *sources* of test anxiety and *expressions* of test anxiety. We scrambled the items purposely to avoid biasing your answers. What is needed now is to pinpoint the *sources* of your fears.

Of course the underlying cause of test anxiety is fear of a negative report. But what specifically is it about tests that gives rise to this fear? Once you have identified these specifics, the way to counteract them will be clearer.

There are four main sources of test anxiety: (1) concerns about how others will view you if you do poorly, (2) concerns arising from threats to your own self-image, (3) concerns about your future security, and (4) concerns about not being prepared for a test.

These do not represent distinct and separate categories. They overlap each other. They are focuses of emphasis rather than categories. All four are probably operating to some degree within you.

Let's consider the first source, concerns about how others will view you if you do poorly. The following items of the checklist pertain to this source (3, 10, 17, 25, 32, 41, 46, 47). Return now to the list and see which of these items you have checked. Place the number of each one you checked in the appropriate area of your Analysis Chart on page 14. For example, if you checked items 3, 25, 41, and 46, enter those numbers in row 1 of the chart as follows:

Checked item numbers

1	Concerns about how others will view you . . .	3, 25, 41, 46

The second source, concerns arising from threats to your own self-image, is represented in items 2, 9, 16, 24, 31, 38, 40. Again look back to see which of these items you checked and enter the numbers in the chart as before.

Follow the same procedures for the two remaining sources. The third source, concerns about your future security, is defined in items 1, 8, 15, 23, 30, 49; the fourth source, concerns about not being prepared, relates to items 6, 11, 18, 26, 33, 42.

At this point you are ready to analyze the sources further by considering questions such as: How would I summarize my reactions to each of these sources? How strong are each of these sources of test anxiety for me? Which sources contain things that I can identify with most?

TABLE 1.
YOUR ANALYSIS CHART

Checked item numbers

S O U R C E S	1 Concerns about how others will view you if you do poorly	
	2 Concerns arising from threats to your own self-image	
	3 Concerns about your future security	
	4 Concerns about not being prepared	
E X P R E S S I O N S	1 Bodily reactions	
	2 Thought disruptions	
	General Test Anxiety	

To help you answer these questions go back and reread the items you checked for each source. As you read, imagine yourself in the scene or situation described.

Next you must summarize the strongest aspects of your responses to each of the sources. Doing this will cause you to confront the problem head-on instead of engaging in ostrichlike denial.

14   For example, one person, after considering

the first source, said, "My biggest problem in this area is that I don't want to disappoint my parents. They are counting on me to win a scholarship and the result of this test is vital." Another person said of the same source, "When it comes down to it, I just don't want to look stupid to my friends and other people I know."

For the second source, an individual related, "Here, my main problem is in disappointing myself. I have a high regard for myself when it comes to taking tests. Perhaps too high. If I did poorly on a test it would really upset me. I can't stand not being at the top in test results." Another said, "Of course I'm not the smartest person in the world. But I'm not the dumbest either. I just want my score to reflect my own self."

For source number three, a student said, "I have mentally tied my test performance to my future career and the security and happiness it will bring. I think I may have overdone it a bit."

Finally, this personal summary was received for the fourth source: "Come to think of it, I have never really gone into a test feeling that I had done all I could to prepare. Even when I study my head off, I still have this haunting feeling that I've left something out."

Your task now is to complete the following sentences:

1. The strongest aspects of my responses to source number one are

_____

_____

_____

_____

2. The strongest aspects of my responses to
   source number two are

_____

_____

_____

_____

3. The strongest aspects of my responses to
   source number three are

_____

_____

_____

_____

4. The strongest aspects of my responses to
   source number four are

_____

_____

_____

_____

The second broad category of items in the
checklist refers to *expressions* of test anxiety.
There are two types of expressions: (1) bodily
reactions and (2) thought disruptions. Aware-
ness of these expressions is an important
component of your analysis.

The following items describe various bodily
reactions: 5, 12, 19, 27, 34, 39, 43. Look back at
each of these items as you did above and record

the number of each one you checked in your Analysis Chart.

Everyone reacts physically to taking a test. The nervous system triggers many small, sometimes undetectable (by ordinary means) responses in the muscles and glands. There are no exceptions to this.

To acquire control over these responses we must understand the nature of anxiety. This emotion is a compound of physical and mental processes. A threatening situation plus the accompanying muscle and gland reactions produces anxiety.

Anxiety is acquired in five stages. First, we are conditioned to become anxious in the presence of certain stimuli. Second, when a situation arises that we recognize as threatening, we respond with our bodies (muscles, glands, and nerves) by preparing for flight or escape. Third, insecure feelings become a factor because we feel the muscle tension, gland secretions, and nerve signals (perhaps at an unconscious or low conscious level.) Fourth, these body reactions are disagreeable sensations which we want to be rid of. During tests, signals go to organs to do things that hinder rather than help. The stomach cramps when it should relax. The heart races irregularly when it should beat slowly and regularly. The muscles contract when they should be calm. Fifth, all these reactions create motivation to find relief in safety. If relief cannot be found in reality, we sometimes attempt to find it in fantasy.

If for any reason you cannot run to safety or find some other relief, you are frustrated and a feeling of anxiety builds up and reverberates or echoes throughout your system. Brain-body misbehavior causes havoc.

You eliminate anxiety when you stop the process at any of the five levels. Later we will show you how it can be stopped. Test anxiety will dissipate when you learn self-control.

The second type of expression is thought disruption. The following items describe various thought disruptions: 4, 13, 20, 21, 28, 35, 36, 37, 48, 50. Look back at each of these items and record the number of each one you checked in your Analysis Chart.

When people are continually interrupted in their thinking on tests by irrelevant occurrences (noises, movement, etc.), it is symptomatic of test anxiety. Their psychological readiness is defeated from the outset. They approach the task with all the mental firmness of a wet noodle. Their motto seems to be: "If anything can disrupt my attention, it will."

As you review your thought disruptions, try to remember the last test session you were in. What were some things which you allowed to divert your attention? In Chapter 2 you will learn how to handle thought disruptions.

Finally, there are several items (7, 14, 22, 29, 44, 45) which refer to general test anxiety. General test anxiety arises from a combination of the other sources. It serves as an indicator of a general lack of confidence in taking tests.

Survey your responses now and enter them in your chart. Notice upon rereading the items that they refer to the total test situation. Here is a good opportunity for you to examine your attitude toward tests in general. If you checked several of these items or can identify strongly with one or two, it is likely that several of the sources and expressions have been stewing within you and the resulting brew is distasteful. In the next chapter we will show you how to "sweeten the pot."

SUMMARY

In this chapter you have analyzed your test anxiety. Perhaps for the first time in your life you have reduced it to its component parts in an orderly way. You have faced honestly some of your emotional tendencies and nervous responses which have been lying beneath the surface causing trouble. But analysis is not enough. Now you must address the solutions based on what you have learned. In Chapter 2 you will learn new ways of thinking and reacting to counteract and eliminate test anxiety. You will gain control and confidence in taking tests. You will also find improvement in your test performance!

What to Do About Test Anxiety

In this chapter we will show you how to develop weapons for taking action against test anxiety. You will learn the mental martial art of combating negative self-statements. You will learn the technique of desensitization and its powerful component, counter-conditioning. With these artillery, plus a number of small-arms concepts from modern psychology, you will no longer need to be defensive in dealing with test anxiety. Declare war. Your nervous sytem will become your ally instead of your enemy.

THE PROPER MOTIVATION FOR READING THIS BOOK

The first thing to do is to ask yourself this question: "What is my real reason for reading this book?" Stop reading now and answer this question . . . . Many people will begin to read this book out of fear. They fear tests and want to make them less threatening. Some people are looking for an easy shortcut to higher scores. We want you to have a broader and more positive motivation for reading this book. You are a worthwhile human being with a life to live and a contribution to make to yourself and others. You deserve to give yourself the best shot at demonstrating or finding out your ability. The goals you have (professional, educational, recreational) are worth pursuing. You are not looking for gimmicks to get a higher score than you deserve. Although tests may make you anxious, you are not reading this book because you are afraid. You are trying to intelligently help yourself because you basically believe in yourself and your goals regardless of your present level of skills or development.

There is an important reason for starting with the proper motivation. It is known, from psychological experiments, that our actions tend to intensify our underlying motivations. If you do the kinds of mental and physical actions we are going to teach you because you fear tests, then your fear would only be increased. If your motivation is to get a shortcut gimmick to a higher score than you deserve, you would be disappointed. If, however, you have the more worthwhile motive of gaining honest, straight forward self-assistance because you basically believe in yourself, then such a motive will be reinforced by the techniques you will learn.

ARGUING AGAINST NEGATIVE SELF-STATEMENTS

As we saw in Chapter 1, people who feel nervous about tests act in two ways: (1) they say negative things (or pose threatening questions) to themselves, and (2) they react physically to these anxiety-arousing self-statements. In order to get rid of test anxiety, both components must be attacked.

Let's consider the first component: *negative self-statements*. In this part of test anxiety, people habitually say things about themselves, in relation to their test performance, which are negative in character. Sometimes these words are spoken to others, but mostly they are said rather unconsciously to oneself. Here are some of the things people do with negative self-statements: they forecast a poor performance, they divert their attention from the task at hand (namely the test), they exaggerate possible negative consequences, they berate themselves when comparing themselves to others, they begin to doubt or deny their own worth as a person, and they deny that their goals are attainable or worth attaining.

There are countless examples of such negative self-statements (sometimes phrased as questions):

1. "I know I am going to do poorly on this test."
2. "I hate tests. They make me so nervous."
3. "I could never study enough to do well on this test."

4. "The others are brighter than I."
5. "I can't concentrate. What's the matter with me?"
6. "What if I flunk this test?"
7. "If I don't do well on this, I'll never reach my goals."
8. "I couldn't eat anything today. I wonder if I'll run out of energy or get sick during the test."
9. "I wonder if I'll be able to relax once the test begins."
10. "I hope there are no 'gum poppers' in the room."
11. "I should have crammed more for this."
12. "Maybe I should have taken more aspirin."
13. "Is there any way to reach my goal without a high test score?"
14. "Maybe I should just try for something else."

Dwelling on such feelings arouses protective responses in our bodies for which there are no appropriate outlets. Therefore they are retained inwardly, causing trouble. This first component of test anxiety, negative self-statements, relates to the psychology of expectations and, specifically, to the more familiar term "self-fulfilling prophecy." You need to understand this concept.

If we expect a certain event or outcome to occur, our expectations may help to bring it about. If we expect someone to steal from us, then our expectation may give rise to guarded, protective, suspicious, and mistrustful behavior of the sort that may attract a thief.

Similarly, if a teacher has some preconceived notion that a particular student is "not bright" and will likely fail (a notion perhaps derived from the teacher's conversation with other teachers), then that student's actions are likely to be interpreted in light of the teacher's "mental set." If the student does poorly, it confirms the teacher's prejudice. If the student does well, it is surprising, "probably a fluke or momentary stroke of luck," or "he must have cheated." The student may have to do better than the teacher's expectation many times to counteract such a prejudice.

If you predict that you will do poorly on an exam when you really do not know the outcome, the negative self-prejudice might cause you to be less alert and put forth less effort than you otherwise might. Or you might be so upset over the prophecy that you can't concentrate. You may direct your energy into "escape thinking" and thus may fulfill your own prophecy unwittingly.

We are not suggesting that you do the opposite: expect a higher score than you deserve. The danger here is that you may devise expectations which give only the illusion of self-control and well-being. Instead we are advocating that you be realistic in your self-assessment.

How can you realistically combat negative self-statements? First you must learn to be aware that you are making them. Many test takers make negative statements so habitually that they are unaware of them. Let your physical and emotional feeling be your guide initially. Feelings often have a way of "leaking" into the musculature (muscle system). If you have any nervous turns of the stomach,

24

facial muscle sensations, or mental revulsion (like saying "oh no!" or "ugh") after having been told of an upcoming test, then you probably have been or will be making some negative remarks to yourself unconsciously. You will learn to deal with physical reactions later in this chapter, but for now they can serve as an indicator that you have been engaging in negative self-statements.

Your main objective is to bring these negative attitudes to the level of consciousness merely by making the mental effort of putting them into words. That is, formulate them into sentences as in the examples given earlier. This beginning step will make them clearer to you.

Next you must learn to make it a habit to challenge negative self-statements. Challenge their *truth*. See if they are *self-defeating*. Are they *self-fulfilling prophecies?* Are they *distracting?* Many of your negative self-statements will crumble and disintegrate when challenges are brought into action.

To illustrate, suppose you have formulated (made conscious) sentences like those in our previous examples. Let's reexamine some of them and see how they might be challenged.

#1. "I know I am going to do poorly on this test."

Truth? I do not know this to be true unless I am totally without preparation (in which case I should arrange to take the test some other time).

Self-fulfilling prophecy? My saying this just might help to make it so. People tend to live up to their negative expectations. At least saying this is not going to help me score my true score.

Distracting? By saying this I will tend to concentrate more on the possible negative consequences than on the test.

#2. "I hate tests. They make me so nervous."

Truth? Tests don't make me nervous. *I* make me nervous! In truth, it is my reactions, which I can learn to control, which make me nervous.

Self-defeating? Pondering this does not help me go into the test with a clear mind. I am already on the defensive.

Distracting? This statement makes me worry more about my nervousness than about the test.

#3. "I could never study enough to do well on this test."

Truth? "Never" is a long time. I am exaggerating again.

Self-defeating? With this idea I have less motivation to try my best.

#4. "The others are brighter than I."

Distracting? There may indeed be others "brighter" than I. Also it is likely that there are others who are less bright than I. So what? I am not really in competition with them unless I make it so in my imagination. Ultimately I am in competition only with *myself* to achieve goals which are appropriate for me.

#10. "I hope there are no 'gum-poppers' in the room."

Distracting? I should not speculate on things like this before the test. If it does occur, I should simply have the instructor or test monitor ask the offender to refrain. After all, I have a right to a suitable test-taking environment.

#14. "Maybe I should just try for something else."

Self-defeating? Maybe so. But I won't know if I should try for something else until after I have the test results and consider the whole situation. In the meantime I deserve to give myself a chance to do my best.

Now take each of the remaining negative self-statements one by one. Challenge them yourself. Apply the test of truth. Ask yourself if it is self-defeating or a case of self-fulfilling prophecy. Is this statement distracting you from the main objective? Formulate your arguments against them.

Write them out on the lines below.

_____

_____

_____

_____

_____

_____

_____

_____

_____

_____

_____

_____

_____

_____

_____

Make it a daily practice to spot, verbalize, and challenge negative self-statements in your thinking. Soon you will have a powerful weapon that will make you better equipped to handle your test anxiety.

YOU MUST RELAX

Earlier in this chapter we noted that people who are anxious about tests say negative things to themselves and then react physically to these anxiety-arousing self-statements. In the preceding section we showed you a procedure for dealing with such negative self-statements. Now we turn to the physical reaction component of test anxiety. Basically what is needed to counteract these bodily changes is training in systematic relaxation and desensitization. This will help you learn how to attack the physical reactions arising from test threats.

Systematic relaxation and desensitization have been used successfully by psychologists and psychiatrists for many years. Using these techniques, they have helped people with phobias, hypertension, and many other nervous system-related problems. It has been discovered recently that individuals, properly instructed, can learn to do this for themselves, and that these methods are successful when used against test anxiety.

You will learn how to use these methods for yourself. It involves your learning only two things: a special type of relaxation and a special use of your imagination. The first thing to learn is how to relax your muscles. This is a simple task, but it does require certain conditions and some determination. Once people experience it, they describe it as "pleasant," "mind-clearing," and "beneficial."

When we use the term *relaxation* as applied to muscles, we mean the complete absence of contractions. When you make any bodily movement (such as raising an arm or leg) you do so by contracting some group or groups of muscles. That is, the muscle fibers "bunch up" or get shorter. This state is called muscle tension. When muscles are completely relaxed there are no contractions whatsoever. The nerves to and from these muscles are carrying no messages. They are like unused telephone lines. The nerves are totally at rest and there is no tension on the muscle fibers. This is the desired state of relaxation for muscles.

The problem is that the state of complete relaxation, the total absence of muscle tension, is not ordinarily achievable. It has been demonstrated scientifically, by means of precise measuring instruments, that even in the reclining person who has been told to relax, some *residue tension* still exists in the muscles. This accounts for the restlessness, slight movements, posture shifts, and slight irregularities in breathing that are experienced by those not perfectly relaxed. Persons in sick beds often experience such restlessness. Such persons have failed to relax away residue tension. Even during sleep, residue tension can be detected (which may be why sometimes sleep is more restful than at other times).

It is astonishing how small a degree of tension can be responsible for not allowing someone to relax completely. The added relaxation necessary to overcome residue tension is very slight, but this slight addition is exactly what is needed. As the person relaxes beyond the stage of residue tension, it has been found that temperature and blood pressure fall, and the slight breathing irregularities are lost. Heartbeat and breathing rate decline. The person lies quietly with lifeless-looking limbs. There is no trace of stiffness anywhere. Even the eyelids become motionless and look toneless. Position shifts of the trunk or limbs are now absent. Emotional activity also dwindles and disappears during this period of total relaxation.

This ordinarily unattainable state of tension release *can be learned*. By practicing the proper procedures a person may attain an extreme degree of relaxation. It has also been found that if a person learns to relax the voluntary muscle system (those you can directly control), then the involuntary system (muscles in the walls of inner organs and viscera) also become relaxed. Emotional reactions then tend to subside. The essence of systematic desensitization is that you allow

30

yourself gradually to become exposed to what makes you anxious or nervous while remaining in a state of consciously controlled relaxation. But we are getting ahead of ourselves. First you must learn the procedures for deep relaxation.

For best results, we suggest that you do the following. Find a quiet place to be alone. Sit in a comfortable chair so you can be fully supported, head to toe (a reclining lounge chair is recommended).

Have the determination that you are going to learn something here. You should read through the entire set of instructions before you actually perform this, so as to be familiar with the whole procedure. Mentally picture yourself doing each step.

The objective is to "turn off" as many external distractions as possible and get your body in a position to be relaxed. The reason for sitting is simply so that you do not fall asleep. Also, it is recommended that you wait two hours after a meal before attempting to relax. This is because the digestive processes may interfere.

Finally, loosen all tight clothing (such as neckties, belts, and scarves) as well as any tight-fitting jewelry. Remove eyeglasses and shoes. Refrain, during this session, from smoking, drinking, eating, gum-chewing, etc.

Now let's begin.

Let your body settle down for a couple of minutes so that it feels entirely supported. After you learn the procedure, it is helpful to close your eyes. What you are going to do in the next few minutes is alternately to tense and then relax muscle groups. Muscles tend to tense up in groups and the correct procedure is to work by groups. You are going to develop a kind of "muscle-sense" in which you can perceive the complete absence of contraction, this stillness of muscles, without trying to hold them still. This is important in achieving total relaxation.

First, begin by bending back the toes of both feet slowly, at the same time, without moving either your ankles or your legs. (Do not lock your ankles or knees, just make no effort to move them.) Bring the toes up and back as far as you can and hold them there until you count slowly to ten (about ten seconds). You will have contracted or tensed a group of muscles for each foot in order to do each movement. Now release your toes slowly and notice the absence of contraction. This is what you are to dwell on for a few moments. Notice the complete relaxation, the "lifelessness" or lack of sensation. Really there is nothing there to feel because we only feel muscles when they are contracting or being stretched. So you are noticing the lack of anything to notice and this is what is important. This *is* relaxation as far as muscles are concerned.

Next, slowly curl your toes downward as if bending them around a small twig. Now you are feeling a different set of muscle groups, those for downward curling. Again, your ankles and knees should not be locked but simply unmoved. After about ten seconds release the tenseness and notice the lack of contraction in these muscle groups. Allow this lack of contraction to continue. Make no effort muscle-wise to hold it. Just let it be.

With the previous muscle groups still in the

their "calmed" state, bend your feet at the ankles. Bend them slowly upward toward your knees and hold them. (Your toes may move somewhat, automatically, but this is to be ignored. They will return to their quiescent state when the ankles are released.) After a slow ten count, release your ankles and concentrate on the absence of tension. The groups of muscles responsible for this movement are now limp as are those for toe movement. Allowing these to remain limp, slowly bend the ankle downward and feel yet another set of muscles come to life and tense up, namely the calves. Hold for ten seconds, then release gradually. Mentally perceive them go "out of gear" and come to rest.

Do not rush the process. Take time to mentally mark the absence of tension in each case. It is very important. If you feel that any groups have again become tense, simply go back and repeat the process for them.

As you can see, we are progressing up the legs; now, with all previous groups still in their limp, "off-duty" state, you are to make the movement of lifting both lower legs off the supporting legrest an inch or so. This will bring into play the muscle groups of the upper thighs from hip to knee. After ten seconds (if you get bored with counting to ten, try the alphabet from *A* to *J,* or say some poetry) release and let your relaxed lower legs go back down to the legrest. What do you feel? Nothing. The muscles of your upper thighs are *doing nothing*. Let them continue doing nothing along with all the muscle groups of your lower legs and feet.

Next we want to get at the muscles on the

backsides of your upper legs. To do this you must press your calves and heels downward against the legrest for ten seconds. The tension will appear in the backs of your legs. Release little by little. Observe how these groups, too, become numbered among the inactive.

Squeeze the two halves of your buttocks together. Your entire pelvis will elevate. Hold—release—observe. Both legs are now completely inert. Mentally scan them. They are, by definition, relaxed.

This may be the first time you ever went about relaxing in this way, that is, systematically. The benefits of this rest will become apparent to you later.

As you continue to sit with lifeless legs and flaccid feet, you are to arch your back so that your stomach and chest stick out. About ten seconds later, release the tenseness. Your lower and middle back muscles become "unstrung" and also pass into the state of doing nothing.

Let's go to the abdomen. Hold your stomach muscles rigid as if to brace yourself for a punch or poke in the midsection. Let go by degrees and mentally follow the gradations of release until you feel no more tension at all. Leave this group, too, in abeyance.

Next, with your arms hung over the sides of the chair arms, bring both shoulders up as far as you can toward your ears and hold for ten seconds. A number of small groups of muscles around your upper body will simultaneously come to attention. Let all these gradually slacken into immobility and remain at ease.

Bring your arms back up to the armrests.

Turn them palms up. Make two fists and bring them up to your shoulders. Squeeze your fists until you feel the tension in your biceps. After ten seconds, slowly return your still-clenched fists to the armrests with the finger side down. Only after ten more seconds of clenching do you totally but slowly let go. Unclench and let your fingers relax naturally. Observe carefully as the tension drains out of your arms and hands.

Most of your large muscle groups are now in a state of quiescence. You have consciously put them in that state and you are consciously allowing them to remain that way. Only your neck and face muscles remain to be "unravelled." They are thought to be especially important in this kind of relaxation. (Shortly, you will be glad you are alone in the room. The spectacle of such distorted and sagging features might give rise to bewilderment or distress in onlookers!)

The neck is complicated. It is like a thick tube with muscles surrounding it, and it is necessary to work on all of these muscles. Remember, we have the front, back, right and left sides. To start, bend your head downward firmly so that your chin is planted against your chest. Hold for about ten seconds and then return it to the headrest. You will have noticed the pull on the back of the neck. This is not tension, but strain which is to be ignored. The tension is to be perceived on the front of the neck. It is here that you are to focus your observations of release. Again, do not be hasty about this work. The benefits are derived from the *slow* perception of tension release and the subsequent mental scanning to make sure the tension is gone.

Next, tension in the back of the neck may be discharged by bending your head back as if to look overhead. The sides of the neck are to be dealt with by bending the head first toward one shoulder (hold—release—notice), then the other shoulder, respectively. Again, be aware of the difference between muscle *strain,* the pulling sensation which is to be ignored, and muscle *tension,* its opposite. Strain is at first more noticeable, but with practice, it can be disregarded.

The face has a rather involved musculature. However, fortunately for our purposes, these too can be liberated in groups by engaging in some rather unsightly distortions.

With the rest of your body and your neck still in limbo, begin work on your face by raising the eyebrows as far upward as possible. After holding, gradually disengage and notice the muscles of the forehead at rest.

For the sake of brevity and because you have, by now, learned the procedure, we are going to list the remaining series of facial contortions for you. Perform them one by one following carefully the preceding pattern (tense, hold, gradually release, and mentally scrutinize each group).

- Wrinkle up your nose.
- Pucker your lips as if to give an exaggerated kiss.
- Produce an extended, intensified grin.
- Grit your teeth (but not too tightly).
- Open your mouth as wide as you can. (After you release, allow your jaw to hang comfortably).

- Squeeze your eyes tightly shut.
- Under relaxed lids, roll your eyes far upward. (Repeat the process for downward, right side, and left side eye movements respectively.)

By now your face should have the look of a deflated football. Let it remain in this condition along with the rest of the muscle groups you have rendered inactive. You may have the sensation of your entire body being suspended, adrift on a sea of repose. Actually, by our definition, you are simply relaxed, greatly so because you have gone about it systematically, but all the same just relaxed. You are in full control. You can terminate this session or continue it at will. It is easy to see that you are not hypnotized, not in some meditative trance state, and not in an artificially altered state of consciousness.

You will become better at this technique with practice. Give yourself a chance to get proficient at it by being patient and following directions carefully.

At this point you may ask, "Now what do I do?" We will answer this shortly, but first let us consider some of the immediate benefits if you were to stop at this point. Obviously when you resume your daily activity you cannot help but be refreshed. You've taken the "ship in for refitting." So this restorative feature justifies having gone through it.

In addition, if you have had an annoying problem, then for a time you have been able to shelve it. And perhaps now you could return to it revitalized. For about thirty minutes you have been preoccupied with an inner consultation with your own musculature. The advantages of getting your mind off your problems are well known. New solutions may have had time to ripen. Old solutions may take on a new light and solidify. You also have not had to rely on sedatives, tranquilizers, or any other drugs.

We think these benefits are real and very useful. But even though you now have learned to systematically relax and have gained the preceding advantages, there is something more that you can now learn to do. This is our ultimate purpose in teaching you to relax. You can learn desensitization.

DESENSITIZATION

Part of the problem of test anxiety is that you become too sensitive to certain aspects of being tested. These provocative features, which we call stimuli, are part of the entire testing and evaluation enterprise. Some of these are physical things and some reside in your imagination. These stimuli have been associated, through conditioning, to your ego-defensive reactions.

Your ego is your self-image. It contains your knowledge of your self and evaluations of your self. It tries to maintain itself as a consistent whole. That is, it tries to keep all the self knowledge and evaluations in noncontradictory relationships with each other. To do this it employs defensive measures.

To characterize what is happening, let us

pick up again on the militaristic metaphor used earlier in this chapter. When something threatens your ego, you either retreat or attack. When the threat to the ego appears to be unattackable, either physically or for social reasons, then ego withdrawal often seems the only recourse. Attending ego withdrawal are such things as: lack of perception, lack of insight, self-doubt, and feelings of inferiority. Some symptoms include: negative attitudes, reluctance, resentment, and the ever-present inner physical reactions which are due to nervous system agitation. You become hyper-sensitive and hyper-reactive. If the threat to the ego appears again, the same conditioned patterns of ego withdrawal responses tend to arise.

But ego threats, unlike physical threats, are basically imagined. They are no less real and no less disrupting, but the skirmishes between ego defenses and ego threats are fought in the imagination. (Note: even physical threats very often have ego threat accompaniments.)

Regarding test taking, stimuli from the physical world, such as the announcement of a test, the test site, or other test takers, may trigger the "battle," but it will be waged inside the mind. Nerve-muscle reverberations and shock waves will extend down through the body.

When "war" is unavoidable (such as when you *must* take a test), and when your reaction is on the withdrawal side, then you go into battle retreating. Defensive maneuvers are given more attention than offensive maneuvers.

There is a reaction chain beginning from

external stimuli to ego threat to bodily reaction. What if we could interrupt this chain? What if the threatening external stimuli ran up against a relaxed body that wouldn't react? What if time and again ego threats failed to hit home? Wouldn't the ego threats begin to lose power and finally exhaust themselves and collapse? Wouldn't the ego have time to "regroup," strengthen, and develop perception and insight? And finally, wouldn't offensive strategies have a chance to be developed?

So far in this chapter we have been using figures of speech which are not to be taken literally. They were used to suggest resemblance to what is actually taking place psychologically. A technique very much like that implied in the questions above is known to psychologists and psychiatrists as *desensitization*. Here, briefly, is how it works. The individual is exposed, by degrees, to anxiety-arousing stimuli while continuing to remain in a physically relaxed state. The effect after repeated sessions is that the stimuli cease to arouse anxiety.

Hierarchies for desensitization are made by drawing up a list of threatening words, phrases, or statements from a general category. In this case it is the general category of testing. These words, phrases, or statements are anxiety arousing. They are the stimuli with which you will be confronted. They are to be arranged in order from lowest to highest in terms of how much anxiety they produce.

Here is what is done with this hierarchy. Each item is entertained in your imagination while you are in a state of relaxation. This is called *counter-conditioning* because it counters things you have already been conditioned to. Only one item from the list, beginning with the least potent, will be imagined at a time. In this way you will be exposed gradually to threatening ideas about test taking that make you anxious. Then you will defuse them one by one until the entire testing enterprise has been drained of its ability to upset you.

We will demonstrate with a hypothetical hierarchy. Later you will be shown how to devise one for your specific needs.

Example Hierarchy for Test Anxiety

1. I hear about some people I don't know having to take tests.
2. Someone I know tells me that he has to take a test.
3. My instructor announces that a small quiz will be given in three days.
4. My instructor announces that a test will be given in two weeks.
5. I am beginning to study for the test (a week and a half before).
6. It is one week before the test and I haven't studied enough yet.
7. It's the night before the test and now I feel fairly well prepared but not totally.
8. I am on my way to the test site.
9. I see other test takers arrive.
10. I see a worried person cramming.
11. The instructor arrives with the test and I wait as they are passed out.
12. I receive the test and look it over before beginning to work.
13. I interrupt the test to think about how well I am doing compared to some of the others.
14. I see the instructor out of the corner of my eye. He is walking very near me.

15. I am baffled by one of the test items.
16. I see some others have finished the test before me.
17. Time is almost up and I am not quite finished.
18. I am talking with others after the test and finding disagreements about certain answers.

So here we have a set of items or stimuli to work with. They may or may not be similar to aspects of testing which bother you, but they will serve to illustrate our point.

Now it is time for your counter-conditioning with the special use of your imagination. Imagery, the conjuring up of vivid mental pictures, is the resource you will tap. As we indicated earlier, much of the problem lies in the imagination. Therefore part of the solution must also involve the imagination. You imagine negative consequences, shortcomings, etc. It is here we must attack. However, you are *not* to imagine the opposite, such as unbelievable success, lucky breaks, or improbably high scores. This is not reality and will in the long run do more harm than good.

We will assume you have gone through the entire systematic relaxation process and that you are well practiced at it and in full control. You have just finished relaxing your eyes as the last step. At this time, while you are still fully relaxed, you are to imagine a scene in which you hear about some people you don't know having to take a test. This is the first item from our example hierarchy. It is the least threatening item in terms of evoking your test anxiety. Mentally and vividly paint the scene around the event. You may be as creative as you desire.

It is partially based on the commonsense notion that you cannot be relaxed and have anxiety at the same time. The two conditions do not go together, as has been demonstrated in laboratory experiments. So if you are totally relaxed (and all residue tension is gone), you will not be anxious.

Yet, you will cease to be relaxed if presented with a highly anxiety-arousing stimulus. If, however, you are first presented with a low anxiety-arousing stimulus while relaxed, you will remain relaxed. The stimulus is not strong enough to break the relaxation. After repeated trials, in which you are successful in remaining relaxed, a still stronger stimulus of the same general category is presented to you so that you may adapt to it. In this way you are exposed to a hierarchy of several stimuli from weak to strong. You adapt to each one, successively, until even the very strong stimuli do not bring about any anxiety responses.

Now you will learn specifically how this technique can be used against your test anxiety. Previously you learned to relax extensively, and to control it deliberately. After you have practiced this several times and gained some proficiency, this state can be used for desensitization. What is needed next is a test anxiety hierarchy.

For example, you might imagine that you are in the hallway of a school. It is a modern building with dark green tile floors and light green walls. During a passing period you overhear some students you don't know, two males and a female, say that they are going to have a test. And that is all you hear. They pass down the hallway and out of your view. Your thoughts turn to the subject of lunch. End of scene.

Now mentally scrutinize your musculature to see if you are still relaxed. If not, return to work on any muscle groups which seem tense and repeat the relaxation process. After you are relaxed again, you may terminate this session and do something else. If you are still relaxed, and the chances are good that you will be considering the mildness of the initial item, then you may proceed to the next item in the hierarchy.

Again, visualize the scene. It may be that you are at home, sitting in the living room. A close friend telephones and in the conversation she mentions she is preparing for a test to renew her driver's license. The topic switches to a picnic for the coming weekend. The phone call ends and so does the scene. Now scan for tension. Based on your decision, either terminate the session or proceed to the next item.

And so it goes, one by one you desensitize each aspect of the testing situation. In the latter part of the hierarchy you will be confronting yourself with ideas which you have predetermined are high in threat value. But you will be thinking about them while remaining totally relaxed. Thus they cannot make you nervous. Doing this many times will deprive the testing situation of the power to arouse anxiety. You will have been desensitized.

If all of this seems a bit farfetched or unreal to you, we would ask you to consider how farfetched and unreal some of your negative self-statements are. We are dealing with the world of imagination, a world which is often farfetched and unreal. But the effects are very often not so remote and are quite real. And too often they are unpleasant. So if the trouble is in the imagination, you have to go there. You will, however, take along some rational artillery. In fact, later in the book we will show you how to make a real ally of your imagination in memorizing for tests.

Here are some suggestions for making and using your own hierarchy. Make up as many items as you feel apply to you. Although the total number of items is up to you, we suggest at least fifteen.

Write them out on the lines provided.

_____

_____

_____

_____

_____

_____

_____

_____

_____

_____

_____

_____

_____

_____

_____

_____

_____

_____

Items can be added, deleted, or switched around if you want. They can be general or specific. They can refer to physical things (like the classroom) or nonphysical things (like a negative attitude). They can be about you or someone else. But they all must be directly or indirectly concerned with test taking.

Also it is helpful to write each one on a separate index card or sheet of paper. In this way you can rank order them in a stack, place them near you before you relax, and then visualize them, one at a time, when ready.

We advise that you consider no more than three items and that you engage in only one session each day. To attempt more is pushing the technique somewhat. Remember, you did not develop test anxiety over night. Distribute your practice and the results will be firmer.

As you begin each new session, go to the item before the one you left off with in the previous session. Remember to terminate a session after any one of the items in the hierarchy disrupts your relaxed state. Begin the next session with the last item you were successful with and then try again with different imagery until you find success with the disrupter. Always try to terminate a session in a relaxed state.

When you have gone completely through one hierarchy, devise another. In this way it is possible to defuse any and all aspects of the testing experience. After desensitization you will not be so hyper-reactive to the testing situation. The threat power of test stimuli will neutralize and fade. Now you are free to develop confidence and devote more energy to undisturbed concentration. You are also ready to take advantage of some test-taking skills that are presented for you in Part 2 of this book. You should be able to see by now that you are indeed a whole person taking a test. You are, as we said earlier, a complex individual with strong emotional feelings, and these feelings must be under control whenever you take a test. Otherwise your score is likely to be lower than your true score. You have learned in this chapter the best ways known for dealing with the emotional side of test taking.

Now you are able to go beyond irrelevant and disorienting behavior and become a Master Test Taker. A Master Test Taker not only is in control emotionally, but also has solid test-taking skills. The Master Test Taker is test-wise, unlikely to be caught unaware of the common pitfalls of an exam situation. In Part 2, you will achieve a more total confidence because you will have the tools of the trade of test taking.

PART II

TEST-TAKING SKILLS

CHAPTER 3

Developing Your Test-Taking Skills

Students continually come to us with the complaint, "I did poorly on the test, and I don't know why." The conversation often proceeds something like this:

Teacher: "Did you study?"

Student: "Yes. I read the entire chapter two times!"

Teacher: "Good. Let me see your notes."

Student: "Uh, well, I didn't think it was necessary to take notes."

Teacher: "Okay. What were the main points covered by the author?"

Student: "Well, there was something about the Civil War. And, well, the North won . . . sort of."

Teacher: "How long did you spend reading the chapter?"

Student: (Beaming) "Fifteen minutes the first time, and only eleven minutes the second time. You see, I 51 have this great new speed-reading technique where I spread my fingers over the page at the top and then make spiral motions, as I read, all the way to the bottom."

Teacher: "I see. How long ago did you start studying for the test?"

Student: (Shrinking) "Last night, at ten o'clock."

Teacher: "I see. Was your concentration interrupted?"

Student: (Regaining confidence) "Absolutely not! I shut the sound off during TV commercials and went at it hard . . . at least until the pizza arrived."

Obviously the student lacks understanding of the testing enterprise. There is no indication of the presence of good test-taking skills. We admit that this is an outrageous case, but it is not uncommon! We trust that you, the reader, are not so far astray.

Yet, even if you have done poorly in the past, you can develop competent test-taking skills. Once acquired, these skills *must* work in your favor. In Part II of this book, four chapters encompass the major areas involved in learning such skills. In Chapter 4 you will learn how to properly prepare for tests. Chapter 5 is concerned with the forms that test items can take. In Chapter 6 you will learn special techniques to help you remember information for tests. Chapter 7 pinpoints for you the essentials of the actual test-taking

situation.

Proper study habits, we believe, are part of the complete test-taking skills category. Before you begin reading Part II, complete the following Study Habits and Test-Taking Skills Inventory. Don't fail to do this because it will accomplish two things. First, it will give you some assessment of your present study skills. Second, it contains many of the topics to which we refer later.

The correct responses are grouped in the Appendix. But before you turn to the answers try this helpful hint. Read Chapters 4 and 5, then return to the inventory and mark the items again in the way you think they *ought* to be marked. Turn to the Appendix and compare your two sets of responses with the correct responses. We believe you will find that your responses after reading the chapters will closely correspond with the correct responses.

STUDY HABITS AND TEST-TAKING SKILLS APPRAISAL

To help you improve your study habits, we ask you to complete this appraisal.

Directions: Mark *T* or *F* at the left of each statement to indicate whether the statement is mostly true or false as concerns you. If you are uncertain, use a question mark for your response. The appraisal will be valuable to you only insofar as you are perfectly honest in responding to the statements.

_____ 1. I do most of my reviewing of course material the evening before an examination.

2. While preparing for an examination, I get nervous, tense, or for some other reason find it difficult to study.

3. I read all the questions on an essay examination before I begin to write.

4. I often have to reread material several times before I understand it.

5. I have trouble picking out the important points in my course reading.

6. I plan out my answer to an essay question on scratch paper before I begin to write.

7. I look up vocabulary words I do not know or word meanings I am not sure of from the context.

8. Except for important quotations, I take notes in my own words rather than those of the author.

9. During a test I get nervous and cannot do as well as I should.

10. I take notes on loose pieces of paper rather than in a notebook.

11. Sometimes I make outlines, diagrams, or charts to represent points in my reading.

12. I don't really know the elements of a complete sentence.

13. I often have to wait for the mood to strike me to study.

14. I review regularly.

15. My studies are frequently interrupted by visitors, phone calls, and other distractions.

16. As a rule, I complete one study assignment before starting another.

17. I spend time that I should spend on my homework at the game, on a date, at the movies, lounging, reading light

fiction, or watching TV and listening to music.

___ 18. Sometimes I sit down to study only to realize that I don't know exactly what the assignment is.

___ 19. I use subject matter learned in school to help me understand events in the outside world.

___ 20. I keep course notes together in my notebook.

___ 21. I have trouble writing conclusions to essays.

___ 22. I inadvertently tend to take down unimportant material in my notes and so I study material not tested.

___ 23. I make an outline or plan for a report before I start to write.

___ 24. I take notes after I have completed my course reading rather than taking notes on each point as I read along.

___ 25. I usually complete my reports several days before they are due so that I can proofread them and rewrite them if necessary before submitting them.

___ 26. I sometimes don't have reports ready on time, or hurriedly do them if I am forced to have them in on time.

___ 27. I dislike certain teachers or courses and it interferes with my scholastic achievement.

___ 28. I often discover that I have read several pages without knowing what I have read.

___ 29. I often skip the tables and graphs that I find in my reading.

___ 30. I mark important or difficult passages in my books, so that I can give specific attention to these points when I review.

_____ 31. I keep a card system or indexed notebook for recording new vocabulary words and their meanings.

_____ 32. I pause at breaks in my reading, such as at the end of a chapter, and recite to myself the chapter's main points.

_____ 33. When I have problems with my work, I do not hesitate to talk them over with my teacher.

_____ 34. I sometimes pronounce words to myself as I read, by muttering to myself or moving my lips.

_____ 35. I feel that teachers are unsympathetic toward me.

_____ 36. I am often afraid to recite or answer questions in class even when I know the correct answer.

_____ 37. Frequently I do not get enough sleep and feel drowsy in class.

_____ 38. I make use of new words in situations where they apply.

_____ 39. I have a definite study schedule, with times and places for studying.

_____ 40. I have a tendency to daydream when I am studying.

_____ 41. My study periods are often too short to get warmed up so that I fail to focus on the task of study.

_____ 42. I review previous material before beginning to work on an advanced assignment.

_____ 43. I stick to my study plan except for good reasons.

_____ 44. I sometimes study while watching television or while people are conversing in the same room.

_____ 45. I spend too much time on certain course work and not enough on others.

_____ 46. When studying, I often get up, walk about, read from the newspapers, or get a snack.

_____ 47. I think out specific examples to illustrate general principles or rules that I have learned.

_____ 48. I have trouble getting down to work at the start of a study period.

_____ 49. I sometimes get to class or sit down to study only to find that I did not bring the necessary books, pencils, notes, or other study items.

_____ 50. I make use of facts learned in one course to understand other subject matter.

_____ 51. I sometimes "overlearn" material; that is, I work beyond the point of immediate recall.

_____ 52. I really do not know how to start an essay.

_____ 53. I worry about my course work.

_____ 54. When preparing for a test, I sometimes try to memorize the exact words from the book.

_____ 55. I read by indirect light rather than by direct light.

_____ 56. I skim over and make an initial survey of a chapter (for example, by reading the paragraph headings) before tackling the material in detail.

_____ 57. I feel that the teachers are my friends.

_____ 58. For the most part, I find my school work interesting.

_____ 59. I study for most exams with the idea of remembering the material only until the test is over.

_____ 60. I read rapidly enough so that I can cover my assignment quickly but thoroughly.

Now read the rest of Chapters 4 and 5. When you finish return to this completed inventory and closely analyze your answers. What are your strengths? Weaknesses? In what areas do you need to work on bad habits to turn them around? How much work does each area need? How should you accomplish your aims? Answer these questions and you will be on your way to good study habits.

CHAPTER 4

Preparing for Tests

Psychologists recognize that regardless of intelligence or knowledge some people tend to do better in test situations than others. They know that those people work better under stress. It is also true, however, that some people score higher because they are test-wise. These people are aware of test preparatory techniques and take advantage of their test-taking knowledge to score as well as they can.

In this chapter you will fix your attention on developing your test preparatory techniques. You will learn the where, when, and how of proper study for tests. You also will acquire the proper habits relating to study and test taking.

WHERE TO STUDY

Concentration is a vital key to learning. Concentration means total attention to the matter at hand. To have good concentration you must focus on the subject material and blot out everything else. Distraction is the major barrier to developing your concentration powers. You, therefore, should strive to 59 achieve a study environment as free from distractions as possible.

Students will often produce their own distractions. One student we know always studies in the cafeteria at the student center. He says he feels better when he has people moving and making noises around him. But he never seems to get much homework done. When pressed he admits that he gets very little accomplished. "I just can't stand to be cooped up in a quiet room," he says. He also admits that he lacks study discipline. There is no research which shows that background music, television, or any other noise can help you study more successfully. Background music may be helpful to people doing monotonous, routine jobs in factories or offices because it takes their minds off their work, but you are only fooling yourself if you think that music will relax you and make it easier for you to study.

Noise is the number one contributor to poor concentration. Others include: interruptions, too much comfort, inappropriate room temperature and lighting, and lack of organization.

INTERRUPTIONS

There are two types of interruptions: those originating from outside sources and those originating from you yourself. Telephone calls, visitors, and roommates or family members are some of the most common sources of interruptions to be avoided. These can be partly controlled or eliminated by finding a good study location. You should pick out three different spots, such as the library, dorm study room, student center reading room, etc. The most serious interruptions, however, are caused by oneself. Getting up to get coffee, pencils or pens, more paper, and the like is self-defeating and, for the most part, avoidable. Try this: place a pen in another room and walk in to get it five times in succession. This will be so monotonous that it may cure you of the problem. Get organized so that you do not get up except for periodic breaks (a five-minute break every hour is advised). You may wish to place a timer or clock radio behind you (so that you don't constantly look at it); and don't get up until the alarm goes off or the clock radio goes on. Ask others where you live not to disturb you. Have someone take phone messages, and then return calls later. Note anything that you don't want to forget and attend to it later.

Almost every study environment has some small, unavoidable distractions. You, however, can learn to disregard petty annoyances. If small things really bother you (for example, light traffic outside your window), you must become aware that the real source of distraction comes from your inability to disregard petty stimuli. The solution is to get into the work by "tuning-out" these minor disturbances.

Focus your total attention on the work. Your environment will be free of small distractions when you develop an enthusiasm for learning and break up negative study habits. Otherwise, no environment will be distraction free.

COMFORT

A study spot which is too comfortable (for example, a stuffed chair) may bring on sluggishness or drowsiness. Make yourself comfortable (an uncomfortable seat can be a distraction as well), but not too comfortable.

TEMPERATURE

Regulate the room temperature so that it is a bit cool (if need be, wear a sweater), but avoid a cold environment. Sixty-five to seventy degrees seems to be the best temperature range for most people.

LIGHTING

Lighting should be arranged so that you do not tire your eyes by glare or squinting. Many reading authorities consider over-the-shoulder direct lighting to be best. If eye problems persist, seek medical advice.

ORGANIZATION

Lastly, organize your study materials and desk or table area so that you do not have to get up or strain to reach essential study materials. Neat surroundings engender an orderly mind and promote accurate work.

WHEN TO STUDY

The first thing you must decide is whether or not you really intend to study! Many people sit down to study without any real intention to do so. They are only going through the motions because they have scheduled themselves to study at a certain time. Psych yourself up to study! Set goals. Have a study purpose. A proper study schedule and self-discipline can lead to productive work. One way to keep yourself at your study desk is to pay friends if they catch you *not* studying during your scheduled time. (An acquaintance of ours lost five dollars and a bad habit using this technique.) You must have knowledge to score high, so set your mind to achieve learning goals.

Below we have reproduced a sample study schedule for your use. Use it wisely and you will see profitable results coming from it. As was said earlier, schedule a break from your studies every hour or so. It helps to refresh the mind. A schedule is an organizational tool meant to help you get work done. You also will find that you will have more free time with a schedule. Without one it is easy to waste your valuable time needlessly.

In the spaces below abbreviate your schedule in the following manner: M = math, A = art, H = history, SP = study period, C = class, L = lunch, F = free time, etc. Now, fill in your schedule for the week. Give it a chance for the semester and stick to it nine times out of ten. It will make a big difference. Your study habits will greatly improve and so will your grades.

TABLE 2.
SAMPLE STUDY SCHEDULE

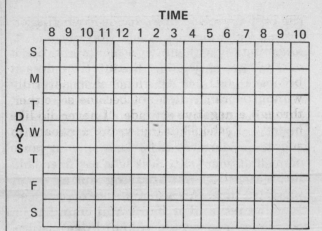

TIME

	8	9	10	11	12	1	2	3	4	5	6	7	8	9	10
S															
M															
T															
W															
T															
F															
S															

DAYS

Everyone has different times during the day when he/she studies best. Research indicates that morning and early evening hours are the most productive periods for most people. But so many variables are involved that you will have to find out your best study hours. Don't force yourself to study when you are tired. Fatigue often carries with it negative attitudes. You cannot study effectively when you are tired. With proper planning you can avoid studying when it is not conducive to productive learning. Plan ahead! Do not waste time by just going through study motions.

HOW TO STUDY

START WITH A PROPER ATTITUDE

Learning subject matter is hard work. But it can be very enjoyable. Really. How does it become enjoyable? It does not come naturally without work. It does not become so, either, through a negative attitude. "I never did like history in school" is the wrong approach to successful learning. Don't feel limited because of a certain teacher you did not like. "My history teacher was an old witch and all we did was take notes from the book." Open your mind to all subject fields and give them a chance. As we mature our likes and dislikes change, often drastically. History, as presented in college, is decidedly different from, and more sophisticated than, high school history. The point is you have to get into it before you can get anything out of it. Deep and genuine interest in a subject seldom comes before effort in that subject.

Some people will go through their college history courses in the same way that they went through high school history and with the same attitude. They will get little out of this learning opportunity. But people with a more mature attitude toward learning will try to fully understand the material, and they may find that they have gained more insight into the world around them and its workings because they have learned how today's world came about through history. Learning sparks interest and someone who has learned will in most cases enjoy the subject more.

Attitude and concentration go hand in hand in the learning process—they are the essentials. But there is more to the complete student than just attitude and concentration. And you can get there! If you follow common sense, acquire and maintain a mature attitude, work diligently, and develop good concentration, you will be the Master Test Taker.

DEVELOP GOOD HABITS

Habits can help you to tackle study problems systematically. They also can prevent you from solving problems. Habits can be faithful servants or cruel masters. Sloppy practices and disruptive patterns can put you in a state of general disarray. But you can build healthy, practical ways of preparing for tests. By practicing techniques and approaches and developing proper attitudes, you can establish good habits, all of which will contribute to the skillful handling of exam preparation.

We have covered some of this ground in the above sections. Now you must practice these habits (for example, concentration, careful reading, etc.). Perhaps a good way to start is to practice on less important tests. If you study for a classroom quiz with calmness and clearmindedness, you have a jump on being able to properly study for other tests. Practicing good habits will generalize to more important examinations as well.

One final point about habits: When studying or taking a test, be conscious of drifting off to other thought regions and snap back to the task at hand. Develop strong "snap-back" power.

HOW TO STUDY

REPLACE POOR READING HABITS WITH GOOD HABITS

Have you tried your best to improve your ability to read? In most cases, readers answer no. Yet practically anyone can substantially increase his reading rate. In fact, many readers can double their reading speed without loss in accuracy. No speed improvement secrets exist. All it takes is a few reading skills and work. You provide the work and we will outline the skills you need to acquire. If you have the will to improve, we will point the way.

You can use the reading technique of *skimming* to your advantage. It may be used to save time under certain circumstances. But it is a very limited tool. Skimming is best used to review material or in searching for specific information in your reading. The lasting structures of improvement, however, cannot be given to you; they must be built inside yourself, from the foundation to the roof, through concentration and will power.

"I read the chapter three times and I still failed the test" is a common student refrain. Some students read the material only once or twice and "ace" the exam. Do they have photographic memories? No. There is no such thing as photographic memory. The brain does not record information like a camera. Do they have fantastically high IQs that make them innately knowledgeable? "Jack gets all A's and doesn't even study!" This, of course, is a myth. How do they do it? The answer is that they do it right the first time. They read efficiently. There is an old Mexican saying that applies here: "The lazy man works twice." It is not how many times you read the material that counts, but how you read it. Quality counts, not quantity.

A principle of good reading is that you cannot read slowly and read with good comprehension. To read with good comprehension, you must read efficiently. Reading too fast is also in opposition to efficient reading. So what is an efficient reading rate?

Let's start with what is *not* an efficient reading rate for perspective purposes. It is not reading everything evenly. More of the material will be remembered if everything is not given equal emphasis because every word of the material is not worth remembering.

All reading matter ought not to be read rapidly. If you read your philosophy or science lesson at 400 or 500 words per minute, without pausing for reflection or unfamiliar terms, you would be wasting your precious study time. When dealing with abstract subject matter, you must work slowly enough to comprehend concepts and terminology.

If an efficient reading rate is neither fast nor slow, what is a proper reading rate? It is one that suits your purpose. When studying science, you may read under 200 words per minute. When reading a novel, you may read over 400 words per minute. Your speed depends on your purpose, your previous knowledge of the subject, and the difficulty of the subject matter.

Your reading rates will vary with your purposes. If you read for specific details, your rate will be slower. If you are looking for general information, your speed will be faster. If your purpose is to find another or a particular point of view, your rate speeds up. Ascertain your purpose before you begin your reading.

You might ask yourself a few questions to determine your purpose: What does the teacher want me to know for the exam? What is the author trying to say about a particular subject? What do these words and ideas mean? How do these ideas relate to previous ideas in the book?

Slow readers usually have several bad reading habits, not just one. A typical fault is vocalization; that is, the reader's belief that he must pronounce every word. Your speaking rate is often less than half your reading rate. So pronouncing words to yourself out loud or silently slows down to a crawl any potential reading rate you might have set as your goal. Chew gum or put a pencil between your teeth to help cure yourself of this habit. Another common error is using your finger, pencil, or ruler as a reading guide. This unnecessarily focuses your attention on the location of words and not on what the writer is trying to communicate. Make your eyes do the work, not your fingers. Do not move your head with the words. This slows your reading rate down to the rate you move your head. The idea is to increase the visual span your eyes can take in, and other physical movements can only hinder your effort.

One further piece of advice: Be aware that eye movement must progress or move forward, not regress or move backward. Regression takes place when the reader stops and backtracks to reread a part or to pick up a word that he has missed. Even good readers regress on occasion, but poor readers do it frequently, making it a bad habit.

Eye movement is a series of short stops or pauses during reading, not a smooth visual action. Reading authorities call these pauses *fixations*. The number of fixations indicates your reading speed. The fewer fixations you have on a line of print the faster you may read. When your eyes "fix" on a spot, the word group seen is called a *recognition span*. It is made up of two or more words. Your aim should be to increase your recognition span and decrease the number of fixations you have per line of print.

Read for thoughts, not words. Word groups tend to form thought units. A fast reader sees word groups but registers thought units in his/her brain. Thought units are natural blocks of understanding through which the theme of the sentence is developed. What forms do they take? There may be a noun and its adjective, a subordinate clause, a prepositional phrase, a relative pronoun and its verb, etc. Here is a simple sentence and its thought units:

There *is no* such thing as a *charitable miser*.

If you can read simple sentences with two or three fixations, you will be able to read quickly and to follow the author's ideas easily. Then you can work to reduce fixations on more difficult reading materials. By working on this objective you will increase your reading speed dramatically.

70   Most high schools and colleges provide free

reading laboratories with qualified personnel for their students. It may be to your advantage to use these facilities if you feel you need them.

Some people approach books with pained anticipation. They expect difficulty in starting and completing their work so they fulfill this expectation by developing a negative attitude toward reading. If this seems to fit you, the solution is to turn this negativism into positivism. Start with an intent to make the most of your reading. Attack your studies with a determination to get the reading done systematically and eagerly. The author, remember, is trying to communicate *with* you. He is not pitching his material *at* you; often he is telling you about something for which he has a passionate love. View an author as someone who wants to share his observations, ideas, and expertise. He has worked long hours to put his work together for you. When you come to realize this, you should acquire a more positive attitude toward your studies. So respond as you would to an interesting conversation—with interest, attention, and a willingness to learn. Then you will be on your way to reading success.

You can refine your habits by simulating the test situation. If, for instance, you are going to take the SAT or ACT college entrance exam, pick up the Barron's review book. Barron's Guidance Library includes test preparation books covering every major standardized entrance examination. Your high school or college counselor, library, or bookstore may have copies. Time yourself when doing a section. Practice working quickly but carefully.

Other study/test simulations will help you. For instance:

1. Work newspaper crossword puzzles to increase vocabulary and synonym/antonym knowledge.

2. Use workbooks of logic puzzles to stimulate the mind.

3. Play word games like Scrabble for word power.

4. Develop expressive abilities by writing (for example, letters to friends and family).

5. Keep a dictionary and a synonym/antonym dictionary (a thesaurus) handy at all times when studying, reading, and writing.

6. Develop vocabulary by using flash cards and vocabulary books.

7. Practice etymology (the study of the origin and development of words) by looking up the meanings of the parts of a word. Knowledge of prefix, suffix, etc. will help you to figure out word meanings on verbal tests.

You must learn to use a dictionary when studying for tests. Here are some words that have appeared so far in this book: *quiescent, refrain, phobia, brevity, residue, component, engender, scrutinize, reverberation, hierarchy, abeyance,* and *musculature.* Can you say what each word means? Are you sure?

If you are like most readers, you will not have taken the time to look up words you don't know. You will have either skipped over them or you will have attempted to divine their meanings from the context. If you did look up the ones you did not know, fine, you have an essential skill. (If you consciously placed a

72 dictionary near you before you began to read,

we beg your indulgence.) If you did not, you lack a basic skill. Why not begin to acquire this skill now? If you do not have a dictionary handy, stop reading and go get one. There may be some words coming up which you will need to look up.

The existential philosophers claim that the only truth in life comes through action (that is, personal commitment), so make a commitment and do something to improve your knowledge and to acquire good study/test-taking habits.

CHAPTER 5

Test Item Forms

There are two basic forms of test items: the objective test item and the essay test item. Regular classroom exams can be composed of either form or a mixture of both. Most college entrance examinations contain only objective test items. Some colleges, however, require an essay exam for admission. We will discuss in this chapter the two test forms in detail and with examples.

An "objective test item" does not mean it is fair and impartial. On the contrary, an objective test item can be very subjective. Why? Because such items are subjectively selected by the test maker, while other possible items from the material are left out. That is why it is not truly objective. The term "objective test item" simply means an item in which the answers are brief and factual. It is a short-answer test with specific answers expected by the test maker from the test taker. It is objectively *scored*. That is, discounting errors in marking, all scorers would find the same right and wrong answers on an exam. We will refer to this form of test item as an objectively scored test item.

Objectively scored test items come in many types: rearrangement questions, short answer, fill in the blank, matching, true/false, and multiple choice. Let's look closely at these

74

types of items. (The answers to these samples appear at the end of this chapter.)

Rearrangement, put-in-order, or put-in-sequence items test chronological knowledge, geography, largest/smallest discriminations, etc. Here is a historical sequence:

Place in chronological order, starting with the most recent and going back to the least recent in English history. Number 1 for the most recent through 6 for the least recent.

____ Harold I ____ George III ____ Prince
                                                      Albert
____ Churchill ____ Disraeli ____ Queen Anne

Short-answer questions call for the completion of an idea or sentence. Complete this quote:

"He couldn't see the forest _____."

Fill-in-the-blank items call for some sort of recall for completion.

Teddy Roosevelt fought in the _____ War.

Matching questions call for multiple answers and thus may count for several points. Since most matching selections are used only once one error can lead to another error. Matching sections can be tricky, so be careful.

Match the author with the book:

____ *Fathers and Sons* (A) Goethe
____ *Sons and Lovers* (B) Conrad
____ *War and Peace* (C) Turgenev
____ *Faust* (D) D.H. Lawrence
____ *Oliver Twist* (E) Tolstoy
                           (F) Dickens

75

A pitfall on a true/false item is the tendency to read into a statement words that are not there. For instance, true or false?

Traveling is difficult during snowstorms.

This is true. The student, however, may "read into" the statement the word *all*. "Traveling is difficult during all snowstorms." This is not true. It is conceivable that traveling is not difficult during a minor snowstorm. The student, however, is responding to the amended item he has in his mind rather than the item on the test. Here is another bit of advice. The test maker may make use of the extreme statement. When the true/false item is put in terms of *never* or *always* it is usually false. Read true/false items cautiously and reason; don't let your imagination lead you astray.

Multiple-choice questions are the most common form of objectively scored test items. Most standardized tests are composed of multiple-choice items. On such questions you are asked to select the *best* answer (that is, the most true) from four or more choices. This means that the best selection available may not be the best *possible* answer, only the one closest to the best possible answer. The wrong answers may have elements of truth and are included to test the preciseness of your knowledge. Sometimes the choice "none of the above" or "all of the above" is put in to challenge the completeness of your knowledge on the subject. Try this selection:

Circle the letter of the correct answer.

Who in the U.S. government declares war on

other nations?

(A) Secretary of State   (C) Congress
(B) President   (D) Supreme Court

The multiple-choice type of objectively scored test item is the most widely used and probably the best because it can be used to measure not only factual knowledge but also understanding of complex ideas. When dealing with the multiple-choice item, use the following criteria to determine your answer:

1. Read and analyze each item carefully to determine what the question truly calls for.
2. Eliminate two or more selections before deciding on your answer. If you cannot eliminate two or more answers, skip the question and return to it when you have time.
3. Use reasonable hunches whenever possible, but don't wildly guess. Draw inferences from the data available in the question. Use the knowledge you have or your reasoning powers to eliminate choices. The "educated guess" can be profitable to you if you use it cautiously.
4. On items involving reading comprehension, read the question *before* you read the paragraph. Underline key words in the questions and then turn to the paragraph. Underline key words and phrases in the paragraph as well. This affords you the opportunity to know what to look for in the reading.

On some multiple-choice exams there is a penalty for guessing. Your preliminary research on the exam will usually indicate what the penalty is, if any. SAT exams, for instance, take ¼ point off per wrong answer. No points are added or subtracted if the item is left unanswered.

In essay exams it is quality that counts, not quantity. It may take a great deal of writing to cover all the points and ideas of an essay subject, but wordy essays are not usually what the test scorer wants to read. The scorer wants a well-organized and well-written essay answer which covers the subject thoroughly, thoughtfully, and which is to the point.

What are the elements of an essay answer? A good essay answer has a beginning, a middle, and an end. The first paragraph of an essay should state your purpose. An example:

> *Nineteenth-century Russian literature was characterized by two philosophical movements: a liberal democratic view of society and human relationships, and a conservative societal view based on a status quo order. In this essay, I will discuss four major Russian authors and their particular views in regard to the above two philosophical outlooks.*

A first paragraph makes clear your thesis and draws the boundaries within which you will discuss your ideas. The middle or body of the paper sketches your ideas on the subject in detail and clarifies your position with supporting material. The conclusion will either summarize what has been said or draw conclusions from what has been shown in the body of the paper. In short, as an old saying goes: "Tell 'em what you're going to tell 'em. Then, tell 'em. And then tell 'em what you told 'em."

A well-written paragraph has the same elements as a well-written essay, but in microcosm. It has a beginning, middle, and an ending. Consider this sample paragraph from Machiavelli's classic work on politics, *The Prince.*

> . . . I say that every prince must desire to be considered merciful and not cruel. He must, however, take care not to misuse this mercifulness. Cesare Borgia was considered cruel, but his cruelty had brought order to the Romagna, united it, and reduced it to peace and fealty. If this is considered well, it will be seen that he was really much more merciful than the Florentine people, who, to avoid the name of cruelty, allowed Pistoia to be destroyed. A prince, therefore, must not mind incurring the charge of cruelty for the purpose of keeping his subjects united and faithful; for, with a very few examples, he will be more merciful than those who, from excess of tenderness, allow disorders to arise, from whence spring bloodshed and rapine; for these as a rule injure the whole community, while the executions carried out by the prince injure only individuals. And of all princes, it is impossible for a new prince to escape the reputation of cruelty, new states being always full of dangers.[1]

[1]Luigi Ricci (trans.), *The Prince,* by Niccolo Machiavelli (New York: The New American Library, 1952), p. 89.

A well-written paragraph begins with a topic sentence which simply states the particular point to be examined. In this case that a good prince must be merciful. A clear topic sentence tells your reader what the paragraph is about.

The middle sentences ought to explain, highlight, or illustrate your topic sentence. Machiavelli uses a historical example to argue that the merciful prince is one who keeps order because, although individuals may suffer from his cruelty, the public welfare will be enhanced. Thus, the middle section will back up, prove, or elucidate your point. This section should be organized logically, and your best statements may come last to strengthen your argument. This may naturally flow into a concluding sentence.

The conclusion may be simply a restatement of the topic sentence or it may draw a conclusion. In the above quote the conclusion is drawn that a new prince must be strong to keep order. A paragraph's conclusion also may serve as a lead into a new paragraph. In this case, Machiavelli's conclusion leads into a further discussion of the merciful prince.

It is obvious that for such a task to be completed you must have thought about the subject and must be very well organized to pull off the feat. You cannot write a good essay off the top of your head.

It is not only what you say that counts, but how you say it. Good grammar and structure are most important. The purpose of an essay is to express ideas in a coherent, flowing style. If the reader is distracted by sloppy handwriting, poor punctuation and spelling, or incorrect sentence structure, the writer will be penalized. The reader can best understand you if the material is expressed in easy to read and neatly presented prose. Sloppy, poorly written essays are not highly valued by scorers.

The secret to good essay writing is organization. Even mediocre ideas look better to the reader when they are presented in an orderly fashion. Before you answer an essay question, briefly outline the major ideas and supports (using key words as a shorthand) that you wish to cover. This may be done on your test paper (in the margin is a common spot) before you begin to write. If you find that you will not finish in the allotted time, outline what you would have said, noting: "if time permitted, I would have discussed the following..." In this way, the grader will know you have a grasp of the material and you may get a higher grade.

In most cases, if you study for all your tests as if they were essay exams, you will be more successful. For essay answers, you must organize facts and ideas, think about relationships, look for implications, and apply material to concepts. Your knowledge of the subject matter, therefore, will be more than just regurgitation.

Points to remember on essay exams:

1. *Time is of the essence.* Each essay answer is allotted a specific amount of time by the test maker. Write a thorough essay but don't make the mistake of spending too much time on any one essay. An outline helps to provide you with limits (thus a time limit) within which you may write. Stay within limits, do not wander off on tangents (no matter how interesting to you), and you will have a good chance of

finishing on time. Do not be caught short of time on an answer you know well.

2. *Answer the easier questions first.* If you don't, you take the chance on difficult essays of forgetting material for the easier ones. It is best to get going and not ponder over an item too long. Anxiety also may set in on difficult questions, impairing your performance on the easier ones.

3. *Try to "psych" out the best answer.* Every teacher has a preferred style and "best" answer in mind. Study the teacher when preparing so that your essay will appeal to the teacher's preference. Your lecture notes will most likely indicate the teacher's particular slant toward the subject matter. You also may simply ask the teacher, well before the test, what he or she prefers.

4. *When working on one essay you may get ideas or inspirations for another.* Jot down these points in a space not used for essay writing.

5. *Write on one side of the exam page* so that you may use the reverse side for later additions you may think of. An arrow or notation will call the reader's attention to the addition.

6. *Try all the questions.* If you find you have time but do not know the answer, start writing anyway. Maybe ideas will occur to you once you start. You have nothing to lose!

7. *Be specific.* Good graders know when you are being vague and will mark you down for it. Always use facts, examples, or back-up information to support your ideas and points.

8. *If time permits, check your essay over for word omissions, spelling mistakes, factual errors, mechanical errors, use of wrong words,*

etc. Be one of the last persons to hand in your test.

9. *Be sure you know precisely what you are expected to do in your essay.* Watch particularly for the following indicator words in the instructions:

a. *Compare* means to show similarities.

b. *Contrast* means to show only the differences.

c. *Criticize* means to point out errors, weaknesses, and strengths.

d. *Define* means to explain the meaning.

e. *Discuss* means to explain, then elaborate, by showing the reasoning or background information.

f. *Explain* means to tell the how or why of something.

g. *Illustrate* means to give clear, meaningful examples.

h. *List* means to catalogue a series of events or items without discussing or illustrating.

i. *Outline* means to write only the main points.

j. *Prove* means to give arguments in support of the proposition being discussed.

k. *State* means to display briefly and clearly without lengthy discussion.

1. *Summarize* means to give a brief review of the main ideas in a concise manner. Do not give detailed accounts of each idea.

Answers to sample questions:

Rearrangement:	6	4	3
	1	2	5

Short answer: "for the trees."

Fill-in-the-blank: Spanish-American.
Matching:

C
D
E
A
F

True/False: True.
Multiple choice: C. The Congress. The president only *requests* that war be declared.

CHAPTER 6

How to Memorize for Tests

We decided to include a special chapter on memory for you because we believe a trained memory is an essential skill in preparing for tests. In fact memory is basic to all learning. It has obvious utility for test items which demand the recall of facts, definitions, or chains of related facts or events. This can be true of both objectively scored and subjectively scored (essay) items. In studying this chapter you will acquire some easy to learn memory techniques that are especially useful for tests.

It is often instructive to consult the ancient sages to see what they have to say on topics of concern to us. Their wisdom has often set the direction for later thinking and research. The study of memory goes back at least to the early Greeks. Let us see what Plato had to say about memory:

> I would have you imagine, then, that there exists in the mind of man a block of wax, which is of different sizes in different men; harder, moister, and having more or less of purity in one man than another, and some of an intermediate quality ... Let us say that this tablet is the gift of Memory ... and that when we wish to remember anything which we

have seen, or heard, or thought in our own minds, we hold the wax to the perceptions and thoughts, and in that material receive the impression of them as from the seal of a ring; and that we remember and know what is imprinted as long as the image lasts; whatever is rubbed out or has not succeeded in leaving an impression we have forgotten and do not know.

... the people with soft wax are quick to learn, but forgetful, those with hard wax the reverse. Where it is shaggy or rough, a gritty kind of stuff containing a lot of earth or dirt, the impressions obtained are indistinct; so are they too when the stuff is hard, for they have no depth. Impressions in soft wax also are indistinct, because they melt together and soon become blurred. And if, besides this, they overlap through being crowded together into some wretched little mind, they are still more indistinct. All these types, then, are likely to judge falsely. When they see or hear or think of something, they cannot quickly assign things to their several imprints. Because they are so slow and sort things into the wrong places, they constantly see and hear and think amiss, and we say that they are mistaken about things ...[1]

[1]Edith Hamilton and Huntington Cairns, ed., *The Collected Dialogues of Plato* (Princeton, New Jersey: Princeton University Press, 1961), p. 901

Plato, with this metaphor, set the foundation for modern memory training. Modern memory experts have gone on to develop processes of memory to which he alluded.

We now know that memory is based on several processes, all of them working together to achieve the end result—remembering. If any one of the processes breaks down, the result is forgetting. The processes of memory are: selection, attention, association, and repetition. We will examine each of these processes and see how your memory can be assisted.

Before beginning, there are two issues we would like to address. First, we do not claim to increase your natural, inborn memory capacity. We doubt if anyone's basic capacity to take in, process, store, and retrieve information can be increased. What can be improved is the efficiency with which you use whatever basic capacity you do possess. We will show you techniques for making tremendous gains in your efficiency.

Second, the techniques learned in this chapter should not be employed as a substitute for deeper understanding of your material. Deeper understanding comes only with reflection and study. The methods learned in this chapter should be considered as a *first* step toward greater understanding. Although these methods will certainly help you on tests (because you will be able to recall much more), they are not, of course, sufficient for complete understanding.

SELECTION

Selection is the process of deciding which material to commit to memory. It has been said that a well trained memory is one that allows you to forget everything that isn't worth remembering. William James, pioneer American psychologist, has said, "Selection is the very keel on which our mental ship is built. And in this case of memory its utility is obvious. If we remembered everything, we should on most occasions be as ill off as if we remembered nothing." [1] We agree. The ability to pick and choose what needs to be deliberately put into memory is especially important when studying for tests.

There are in general two types of tests: teacher-made tests and company-made tests. We will consider each type in relation to the selection process.

On teacher-made tests you will find two types of items: objectively scored items and essay items. Some teacher-made tests contain both types. Objectively scored items will often be concerned with *terms* given in class or in textbook assignments. (A term is a word or phrase which signifies a key idea or main concept.) Such items are relatively easy for the teacher to write and score. They can reliably yield information to the teacher. So any terms and their definitions are fair game and are likely to show up on tests. You must select

---

[1] William James. *The Principles of Psychology,* (New York: Dover Publications, Inc., 1950), p. 680.

these terms for memorization. You must build, for each test, a Selection List.

All terms given by the teacher in class sessions must be put on your Selection List. You must be constantly on the lookout for likely candidates. Write all such terms in your notebook.

Textbooks are written to help make selection decisions. Any terms or ideas appearing in bold or offset type probably should be included on your list. Sometimes important words or concepts appear in lists or summaries at the ends of chapters in textbooks. We will show you how your list can be easily and efficiently memorized.

If your pre-test detective work has revealed that there will be items of the essay type, a different approach is called for. Here your selection of terms must follow the outline of the material. Try to find out which reading or lecture material will be tested by essay items. Also find out as much as you can about the nature of the items. Will you be asked to summarize, state, outline, prove, illustrate, compare, criticize, explain, discuss, or contrast? There are important differences and you may pay heavily for failure to follow instructions. You should make it a habit to be ready to ask questions about the test and material to be tested. Many teachers freely give out such information to the class, *if somebody asks*.

Armed with pre-test information, you can select the key ideas from the appropriate passages or lecture notes. These should follow the outline of the material. Again textbooks are usually helpful giving chapter, section, and subsection titles or headings. Together, these form an outline that you can work with. Once you have selected and compiled an outline, it can easily be reduced to a few words and memorized. Later, in the association section of this chapter, we will show you just how this is done.

The second general type of test is the company-made test. They are usually standardized. This means they have been given to large groups of people of various ages or levels so as to get standards for comparison. They are usually objectively scored. They cover very broad areas. They are often designed to measure abilities and aptitudes such as reasoning and problem solving. You cannot obtain specific information about what material will be tested. If so, such tests would lose their power as standardized tests. Of course as we have indicated in Chapter 4, you can obtain valuable information about these tests and samples of test items which are like those you will actually have. Such sample items will be like the authentic items in *form* but not in *content*. So although such prior information is useful in familiarizing you with the test form, they do not provide material for memorization.

For company-made tests such as: ACT, SAT, GRE, CLEP, and GED, the selection process cannot be used. Therefore, the idea of memorizing for such tests loses its appeal.

But for teacher-made tests you will have a great advantage if you develop the art and habit of selection. Learning to key in on important ideas is a must for competence in test taking. It will also help develop your interest because you will always be studying

with a purpose.

ATTENTION

Now that you understand that you must select what is to be memorized, you must learn to give the right kind of attention to what is selected. Samuel Johnson, the famous eighteenth-century English author, once said, "The true art of memory is the art of attention."[1]

Attention is the process of focusing your perception on the material to be learned. Productive attention must be deliberate and intense. Sometimes we do remember things we barely gave attention to. This is a passive form of attention. But when memorizing for tests a more deliberate rather than passive form of attention is called for. Look back at the second paragraph of our quotation from Plato. The word *indistinct* is used three times to indicate part of the problem of forgetting. People who are forgetful do not have distinct impressions to refer back to for recall. Their attention has not been of the deliberate, focused sort that allows for distinct impressions.

One reason people do not remember things is because they are not ready to pay attention. One must be set to receive information. This is where the attention process breaks down with most people, right at the very beginning. Their minds are too crowded to receive new guests. In order to have good attention, you must have expectancies; that is, something you are looking for. It is good practice when studying to build expectancies by always asking questions before you begin. You must exclude

---

[1]Samuel Johnson. *The Idler,* no. 74.

other thoughts or external stimuli and center your attention on the target.

It is difficult to retain things we cannot understand. Usually you will have some preconceived categories or receivers in which to place information which comes to your attention. You will have, from prior learning and experience, these receivers ready to handle, code, or decode the information in order to find meaning. Information needed for tests is usually packaged so as to fit conveniently into our receivers. It is like finding the "match" for the information somewhere in our files. We bring to bear our vocabulary and concepts to use on the new information to make sense of it. If you cannot make sense, you will have to build sense (for example, by looking up the word in a dictionary, or asking the teacher for clarification).

Attention tends to wander capriciously to irrelevant things. Accept this fact, and you won't be discouraged when it happens. But fight it! When your mind wanders, ask yourself, "What does this have to do with the topic I am supposed to be thinking about?" Learn to snap your attention back to the subject at hand; otherwise, you are wasting valuable time. In general, the longer you attend to a topic, the more mastery of it you will have. The ability of bringing back wandering attention over and over again is at the very root of successful study for tests.

Thus in order to remember anything for tests you must have initial and distinct attention. If the topic is not automatically interesting and captivating to you, then you will have to force attention by borrowing interest from elsewhere. The memory techniques you will learn in this chapter will take care of the attention, interest, and distinctiveness aspects of your memory.

ASSOCIATION

The process of association is making mental connections between concepts or thoughts so that when one is recalled, it suggests the other also. Probably all learning is based on association. You have been using this tool all of your life. It's impossible *not* to associate.

Try not to think of anything but these two lines for one minute.

You may have said, "Alright, I am thinking of these two lines and nothing else." So you perhaps looked along one, then the other with riveted firmness. But then something came tapping softly at the door of your attention. Perhaps some feature began to suggest something else. But you said NO and turned it away. Back to just the lines, more firmly. Now there is knocking at the door. Irritated, you impulsively divert your attention momentarily and discover an absurd thought standing there where the lines should be. They are not just lines now, but the letter *x* with one of its lines extended ... No, it's a cross fallen over ... a sword ... Oh forget it.

See what we mean? Maybe people should be referred to as "associators" rather than learners. When you learn, you are constantly associating new thoughts to old. Categories already established in your mind are related to the new item. The problem is that this is not often done in an organized or memorable way. It is done briefly, just to gain meaning or understanding and then we quickly pass on to something else. There is nothing wrong with this *unless* such information comes up for recall on a test. Then you may find that your learning was much too casual. You may find yourself among those whom Plato says, "... are likely to judge falsely ... they constantly see and hear and think amiss ..."[1]

When memorizing for tests, you must learn to associate productively.[2] One thought produces another automatically. A general rule in memorizing is: *you can remember any new information if it is associated productively to something you already know, understand, or remember.* This is the basis of many memory devices. For example, few people can remember the geographical shape of Venezuela, or Rumania, or most other nations—except Italy. Most people know that Italy is shaped like a boot. The shape of a boot is something already known. The shape of Italy is difficult to forget once the productive association is made. The thought "shape of Italy" produces "boot," and the question, "What country is shaped like a boot?" produces "Italy."

When science students remember the main

---

[1]Hamilton, loc. cit.

[2]Harry Lorayne and Jerry Lucas, *The Memory Book (New York*: Ballantine Books, 1974). Much of the material of this section on association was adapted from the work of the memory expert, Harry Lorayne.

colors of the light spectrum by recalling ROY
G. BIV (red, orange, yellow, green, blue,
indigo, and violet), again one known thing has
produced another when associated. Students
also have imagined homes on a great lake to
remember the five Great Lakes (*H*uron,
*O*ntario, *M*ichigan, *E*rie, and *S*uperior).

These devices are fine, but are limited to the
specific things they were made for. All these
devices, however, have something in common.
They require some imagination and they are
somewhat absurd. If you think about it, you
can see that they work partly *because* they are
imaginative and absurd. Ponder the preceding
sentence a moment, then read on.

Psychologists have shown experimentally
that we tend to remember things that are or are
associated with the absurd, the outrageous,
the ridiculous, the impossible. Absurd things
seem to be innately interesting, probably
because we spend so much time trying to be
rational. Such facts help explain how people
can remember jokes and retell them. Not only
do they remember the joke, but they remember
who told it to them and where. All of this is
through association. How many times have
you heard someone say, "That reminds me of a
joke I heard ..."? Something in their present
mental content *produced* the memory of the
joke because of its productive association with
the absurdity contained in the joke.

You can make use of this ability in remembering anything. Let us restate the general memory
rule given above with an addition. *You can remember any new information if it is associated
productively to something you already know,
understand, or remember in an absurd way.*

As you will shortly see, applying this modified rule will force attention and interest on things selected for memorization. You will be amazed at your previously unused capacity to make associations. The brain is almost limitless in the number of connections that can be formed. You have probably used only a tiny fraction of your ability. We will show you how to give effort and get much more in return from your work.

To begin, let's assume you need to memorize these items in sequence: cracker, dog, telephone, basket, yodel, tire, carpet, cloud, book, apple.

Now picture a cracker in your imagination. The next is dog. It is the new information. Now the rule can be applied. All you have to do is form some absurd or ridiculous picture to associate the two items. You do not want a logical, sensible image.

A sensible picture might be: a dog with a cracker in its mouth. This is not ridiculous. It is possible and, therefore, undesirable for your purposes. An absurd picture might be a huge cracker, ten feet by ten feet, with a 500-pound dog sitting on it. That's crazy, impossible. But picture it anyway in your mind's eye. You must try, just for a second or two. It's the trying that is important.

The next item on the list is telephone. You already know or remember dog. The new piece of information is telephone. Form a ridiculous association between dog and telephone. (We will suggest one. It is better if you form your own, but for purposes of instruction we will continue to give you suggestions. Whether you use your pictures or ours, the important thing is to see the images distinctly in your imagination.) You see a dog pick up a telephone, dial, and talk. Impossible, but memorable! See it, just for a moment.

The next item is basket. Imagine a basket with millions of telephones floating out of it. Stop reading and think of it for a couple of seconds, then read on. You already remember basket. The new thing to remember is yodel. Picture, clearly, a giant basket yodeling. "This is nuts," you say. It is using your imagination. Stay with us.

Next is tire. See a woman yodeling and millions of tires come flying out of her mouth. Remember, it is very important to imagine it distinctly if only for an instant or two. It's how clearly, not how long, you imagine that's crucial.

Now we have carpet. Mentally fabricate a huge carpet made of tires woven together. With carpet stored in your memory, the new piece of information is cloud. Imagine carpets floating in the sky instead of clouds. Carpets are where clouds should be. Next is book. You open a book and dozens of little white, puffy clouds rise out from between the pages. See it happen.

Finally apple. Imagine an apple reading a book. Incredible! But if you picture it you won't forget it.

At this point go back and read over the associations. If you have pictured all ten items clearly, you will be able to recall them in order. The only item that may give you trouble is the first item because it is at the beginning. It is not associated with anything prior to it. The item was cracker. What does cracker make you think of? Now get a pencil and see if you can fill in the following blanks.

_____

_____

_____

_____

_____

_____

_____

_____

_____

_____

Well, did you remember all of them? You should have. If you did happen to miss one or two, go back now and strengthen the association. Then try the list backwards. The last word was apple. What does that make you think of? We believe you will be impressed with yourself.

Now make up your own list of ten words and try the procedure. You'll find that you will be able to recall any list of items forwards and backwards. With practice, you can extend your list indefinitely.

We will now present some questions which are commonly asked by people concerning this technique. We will follow each with a reply.

1. *Why must the mental picture always be absurd or impossible?*

The absurd is memorable—highly so. In

addition the act of creatively associating two things forces you to be initially attentive, one of the processes necessary for memory. The impressions are distinct because you have striven for clarity. They are also interesting to you because you are creating them.

Many people are reluctant to try to create bizarre images. Their hesitancy is probably due to the effects of having been trained and prodded in school to always think seriously and logically when dealing with subject matter. This may be the first time anyone has asked you to reawaken your childhood ability to generate unusual and impossible dreams. It is still there. Make use of it.

2. *Are there ways to make it easier to form absurd images?*

Yes. First make up your mind that you will do it. That's half the battle. Then, there are some guiding principles which will help.

The first one is *replacement.* Try to replace the function of one thing with another. If you were associating potato with boat, you might see a potato floating in water instead of a boat. As another example, a telescope can be visualized flying instead of an airplane.

Have you ever considered what is so captivating about animated cartoons? In cartoons, things are often out of proportion, exaggerated, and action packed. William James indicated that each one of these qualities innately tends to captivate our attention. In cartoons you can see a neck stretched for a mile. You can see a car shrink to the size of a peanut, a rabbit inflated like a balloon, a character blown up with dynamite only to return unharmed, etc., etc.

99

So make your images *out of proportion*. See
not just a head of hair but a head of hair the
size of a haystack. See a man with feet that are
twenty feet long. See a lady with glasses that
are huge—ten feet across.

Learn to *exaggerate* in your mind's eye.
Don't just see one telephone, see millions. See
millions of tires, not just one. Or go the other
way and see a big tree with only one leaf where
thousands should be. See only one seat in an
entire football stadium where there are usually
thousands of seats.

Get *action* in the picture wherever you can. A
dog picks up a telephone and dials. Clouds rise
out of a book. A building walks away.

Finally, if possible, inject some *emotion* into
the scene. Happiness, sadness, romantic love,
hatred, all tend to be very memorable. You
might see a toothpick crying, a screwdriver
hating its work, or a romantically aroused
chair.

3. *Is it mentally healthy to learn by absurd
   imagery?*

One of the authors was teaching this
method to his class. A certain student was
afraid he would go insane if he continued to
form absurd images. The student had heard
that insane people sometimes have hallucina-
tions which seem to consist of absurd thoughts.
The answer to this is, of course, that hallucina-
tions are a symptom, not a cause, of insanity.
Also, the insane person has no control over the
bizarre images. You have control. Without it
you could not be creative and produce the
images and relate them to other material.

One interesting feature of this method is
that after you use the images a few times in

recalling material, they will not be needed.
You will find yourself, after a while, recalling
the material without using the images.

4. *Wouldn't it be easier to just remember
   things logically?*

No. Memory without vivid imagery is to a
great extent learning by rote, a painfully long
and difficult method. Also many things you
must remember for tests are not logically
related. You would spend too much time and
effort going over and over material to be
efficient. In addition, once things are learned
by rote, they are easily forgotten because of the
lack of associations.

5. *Would it help to "paint a mental mural"
   or to form a story?*

No. Do not do this. It is better if things are
associated two at a time. The association
between two pieces of information should be
independent of the association between one of
those items and a new one.

6. *How long can I remember material
   learned by this method?*

You can remember the material for as
long as you want or need to. If you desire or
need to use the material, then you will
remember it. As the material becomes firmly
lodged in your mind, the associated images
fade, and you will remember it as long as you
need it.

7. *If a term or word appears on more than
   one list, will I get confused?*

No. In addition to remembering individual connections, the mind, at the same time,
remembers whole groups. The images called
up by a word for one list will not be confused
with the next word it was associated with on

another list. Your mind will make the distinction automatically.

8. *How do I remember the first item on the list?*

If the list is for a particular class, form an association between the teacher and the first item. You may associate the first item with your textbook or yourself. It really doesn't make any difference. Just make it ridiculous.

9. *How do I remember abstract things which cannot be pictured, such as irrelevant, motivate, or progression?*

When you come to a word or phrase which cannot be pictured, make up a word (or phrase) which sounds similar and which can be pictured. You could change irrelevant to "her elephant." Picture a girl with her elephant. Motivate can become "motor rate." See a motor idling at a fast rate. Or you might see a "motor hate" its hard labor. Progression could be pictured if changed to "pro aggression." See a lot of pros behaving aggressively. Try the following list on your own. Form near-sounding words or phrases. Write them in the spaces to the right.

supplement _____

practical _____

flimsy _____

compulsory _____

threshold _____

egalitarian _____

ardent _____

essay _____

spiritual _____

casual _____

Now associate your new words or phrases, by twos, in absurd ways. Go over your associations a couple of times to firm them up. Do this and you will discover something amazing. You will be able to recall the original list of words, without looking back. The first word was supplement. What did you change it to? What does that lead you to? It led you to the next word, of course, and so it goes.

Now you have learned that any word or phrase can be pictured either directly or indirectly by means of a similar-sounding word or phrase. For comparison, here is what one person thought of for each of the words in the list: supplement, supper mint; practical, practice call; flimsy, film see; compulsory, come pull surrey; threshold, thrush hold; egalitarian, eagle and a terrier; ardent, car dent; essay, I say; spiritual, spirit tool; casual, cash for all. Then the person formed absurd associations between these phrases, two at a time, and the original list was his!

It's really that simple. It only takes about five minutes. Once you do it, you cannot forget it. Some people have remembered lists containing dozens of words. Since there is no limit to your imagination, there is no limit to the number of words you can handle.

REPETITION

The last process of memory which is important for you is *repetition*. It is always necessary to go over material in order to retain it. In general, the more you go over it, the longer you will retain it.

In memorizing by rote, you must go over and over the material many times before you can recall it. To prove this to yourself, try memorizing any list of ten unrelated words without using the method given in this chapter. It is time-consuming, boring, and exhausting.

But the method you learned in this chapter makes a lot of repetition unnecessary. You need only go over your associations two or three times and you are done. If in your first review of your associations, you cannot recall a piece of information, simply go back and strengthen the association. Try this method a few times and prove it to yourself. The more you use it the more efficient you will become. It is not difficult, not time-consuming, and not boring. It works.

Now let us see how these ideas can be applied to test taking.

Assume your instructor has told you that there will be a section of an upcoming test in which you will have to list the executive departments in the president's cabinet. The first step is to form a Selection List. The departments are as follows (alphabetically):

Agriculture
Commerce
Defense
Energy

Health, Education, and Welfare (HEW)
Housing and Urban Development (HUD)
Interior
Justice
Labor
State
Transportation
Treasury

The first department is agriculture. Think of some similar-sounding phrase which will serve to remind you of agriculture. You must make it an object, something "seeable." How about "a great vulture"? That sounds similar and it's unusual. Use exaggeration. Visualize a thousand-pound vulture. That's a great vulture! It will remind you of agriculture.

Next is commerce. Change it to something else. Picture yourself saying the phrase, "come hearse," to a funeral hearse. That will remind you of commerce. Now associate, in some absurd way, "a great vulture" with "come hearse." You might see a great vulture saying, "come hearse." See it in your mind's eye, clearly, just for a second.

The next department is defense. How about changing it to "the fence." Associate "come hearse" with "the fence." Picture a hearse sitting on a fence. See it vividly. Next is energy. let's change this to "in her jeep." A girl you know has a fence in her jeep. Ridiculous, but memorable if you think about it.

Now we have health, education, and welfare, commonly known as HEW. If you have a friend named Hugh, you are in luck. If not, Hugh Hefner (a well-known publisher) will do. Picture Hugh in her jeep. (A little romantic emotion, perhaps?)

Next is housing and urban development, commonly known as HUD. This is easily changed to "mud" (which is commonly found around housing and urban renewal). Can you picture Hugh covered with mud? Mud will get you HUD.

The department of interior follows. Substitute "inner ear." There is mud in my inner ear and I cannot hear. Justice is next. You can picture a huge glass with "just ice." As it melts, I pour it into my inner ear to wash the mud out. Then we have labor. It can be replaced with "lay boards" (action). Into a glass of "just ice" you "lay boards."

For the State Department, you can visualize the shape of your home state. Think of it. What shape is it? Now lay boards, mentally, around the shape of your state. For transportation, use "train station" instead. Your entire state is one gigantic train station.

Finally we have the Treasury Department. Of course you can picture a treasury (a place with a lot of gold bars, for example). But instead of gold, there are piles of trains. It's a train station. (Here we have used the principle of replacement.)

At this time, go back and read through this entire section twice, beginning with agriculture. Picture in your mind each absurd association. To get agriculture, you can picture the president opening his kitchen cabinet only to find "a great vulture" sitting there.

Now write the executive departments of the president's cabinet, from memory, on the following lines.

_____

_____

_____

_____

_____

_____

_____

_____

_____

_____

If you have followed our instructions, you will know them. You will also know them tomorrow and the next day if you like. The only way you will know for sure is to try it. We think you will be pleased with the results. You cannot forget them for as long as you choose to remember them.

Suppose there will be a forty-point essay item on an upcoming test. For illustration, we will use Chapter 1 of this book. The essay test item is phrased as follows: "Summarize the information given about test anxiety in Chapter 1." Summarize means to briefly review the main points of the subject. You are not to give detailed explanations. They will only count against you.

At first this may seem like a difficult task. But notice you are not asked to memorize everything which was said about test anxiety.

You are only asked to summarize the main points. You will be reducing the material down and will have to form a Selection List of words or phrases which are associated with the key items.

Let's try it. It will only take a few minutes. You will learn something you can use all of your life.

Turn back to the first page of Chapter 1. The first paragraph is rather introductory, more to catch interest than to impart knowledge. But the second paragraph contains a definition of test anxiety. The main word in the definition seems to be *nervousness*. That is, the main element in test anxiety is nervousness. This is certainly something we want to select.

The next paragraph is addressed to the issue of whether or not some test anxiety is good for you. The answer is no. It is a negative nervous reaction which does more harm than good. The phrase *negative reaction* will serve to summarize this paragraph. We will add this to our list.

In the next paragraph, characteristics of test anxiety are given. There are six of them. *Characteristics (6)* will serve to introduce this paragraph. It seems that it would be important to include these characteristics in our summary. The word *threat* will remind you that one of the characteristics is a feeling that tests are more of a threat than a challenge. *Worrisome* will remind you of worrisome thoughts about the consequences. *Physical* will remind you of the physical reactions which often accompany anxiety. *Trouble* will help you recall this dual characteristic of having trouble remembering and keeping your mind on the items. The *others* can remind you of worry about others scoring higher than you. *Decreased* is a word which will remind you of the last characteristic.

The material then switches to emotional reactions and how they interfere with smooth, controlled performance. Test anxiety interferes with test performance. The word *interfere* can remind you of this idea.

The main point made by the authors about test anxiety is that it is learned. The word *learned* must be added to the list. Also, it forms a kind of *trap* which we fall into at an early age.

For the sake of brevity, we will simply list the remaining key words for our Selection List. You should follow through the remainder of Chapter 1 and locate the paragraphs from which each of our key words was taken. Here are the remaining words: *pinpoint, sources (4), others' view, self-image, future, prepared, expressions (2), body,* and *thought.*

We have selected twenty-one words or phrases from the chapter that are associated with the main points made by the authors about test anxiety. All that remains is to associate these terms in some ridiculous ways to each other. Here are all of the terms:

nervousness _____

negative reaction _____

characteristics (6) _____

threat _____

worrisome _____

physical _____

trouble _____

others _____

decreased _____

interfere _____

learned _____

trap _____

pinpoint _____

sources (4) _____

others' view _____

self-image _____

future _____

prepared _____

expressions (2) _____

body _____

thought _____

The next step is to form a picture for each term. If you cannot picture a word directly, then change it to something which sounds similar and which can be pictured. Write whatever it is you picture for each term on the line to the right of that term.

The first term is *nervousness*. Being the first term, it would be well to associate it with the subject. Since test anxiety is given in the essay question, it must lead you to nervousness. You might see yourself having an exaggerated case of nervousness (shaking, vibrating, etc.) when you see the term test anxiety in the question. That would be ridiculous if you have practiced the ideas in Chapter 2. Write "See myself nervous" on the line next to nervousness.

Next you must associate nervousness with *negative reaction*. This latter term is difficult to picture, so change it to something else. Try "negative knee-action." You are shaking all over except when you look down at your knee, there is no action, there is "negative knee-action." This will remind you of negative reaction.

The next term is *characteristics (6)*. It can be pictured as "car after sticks." Picture a car chasing after six sticks. Now link "negative knee-action" to "car after sticks" in some absurd way.

At this point we will refrain from suggesting associations. It is better if you think up your own. It forces attention, creativity, and interest. As an exercise, you complete the associations for the key terms of Chapter 1. You will learn more about these methods by actually doing this yourself. You will find that you can handle twenty-one terms with ease. By following the outline of the chapter, the individual terms will cluster and cling like grapes to their stem.

Then try these methods on your own textbooks. Students have told us it's a great help to study, even for multiple choice, fill in the blank, and matching test items. This is because you can acquire the main points of an entire chapter quickly and easily.

CONCLUSION

In this chapter you have learned how to memorize for tests. You can now study for tests with more confidence because you have acquired more skills. You now have a better understanding of memory and its subprocesses. You have learned how to apply this understanding to the business of taking tests. You are becoming a Master Test Taker.

CHAPTER 7

Preparation Immediately Before Standardized Tests

Many students ask, "What can I do just before my college entrance examination to prepare? Should I do further reviewing? I feel that I should spend every hour before the exam getting ready." What can you do just before and during the test to improve your score? In this chapter we will present some "do's" and "don't's" of standardized test taking.

By standardized test, we mean a company-made test like the SAT or ACT that is given to a large number of individuals at test sites all over the nation on specified dates during the year. These tests are used for college entrance, law school entrance, graduate school entrance, medical school entrance, etc. to determine whether or not an individual may be qualified to study in his or her selected field.

In organizing and preparing for a test the little things count as well as the big things. The ill-prepared person puts himself at a disadvantage and may even cause himself to be put in an unnecessary state of alarm. Your 113 aim is to be completely prepared and alert when you arrive at the examination site. Let's start with the day before the test.

Follow a normal routine the day before the exam. "Nothing in excess" ought to be your guide. Avoid too much food, drink, romance, TV, music, exercise, reading, "partying," socializing, etc. On the morning of the test, eat lightly and do not have more than two cups of coffee or tea. In short, do not overstimulate or depress your senses. Overdoing it may cause fatigue and/or nervousness. Get a normal night's sleep and cut any travel time to a minimum, even if you must stay overnight near the test site.

Do not try to cram to fill any knowledge gaps. Some reading is good for the mind the day before the test, but the mind ought to be open and clear. So it is best to do light reading. Preparation books for specific exams, with their sample questions, ought to be consulted, but not the day before the main event. Do not fill your mind in this period with specific clutter of any kind.

Here are some test site arrival tips. Wear comfortable clothing. This is neither a formal dress occasion nor a social gathering. Your aim is to avoid physical distractions to your concentration. Take clothing which may be partially removed if the room is too warm and something which may be added, such as a comfortable sweater, if the room is too cold. Do *not* assume that the test site will be reasonably comfortable. Large rooms, where these tests are conducted, are notorious for their poor ventilation and heating and cooling.

114 Check the room environment. Do not arrive

too soon (sitting around does not help concentration), but arrive before most do so that you may pick out a good spot. Do not sit near hallway doors. Hallways may become noisy and disrupt your concentration. Avoid sitting near drafty windows or in front of heating or cooling system openings. When you sit down make sure you can stretch out; don't be cramped in your seat. In short, your environment ought to be comfortable and should not distract you from your mission.

If you tend to get drowsy during long exams, you might wish to take a candy bar into the exam with you. Often drowsiness is caused by low blood sugar, and a sugar-rich candy bar can temporarily boost the blood sugar to keep the brain functioning at a high level of efficiency. Don't overdo it; one candy bar is enough. The candy's sugar is only good for an hour or so, depending on the person, and over a long period of time it will have a reverse effect. The body reacts to high blood sugar in a way that results in low sugar and possibly drowsiness. So do not take it before the exam. Only use the candy when you feel the need to use it.

Be properly equipped. Too many people come to the test ill prepared. They may end up either begging for a pencil or wrestling with books and papers. Often you are requested to bring two or three No. 2 pencils. Is scratch paper allowed? It frequently is and you should have a few sheets for the mathematics section. Don't forget to bring your admission card and anything else (such as identification) required for entrance. Check the testing service's information booklet for requirements. Avoid unnecessary problems.

Now you should be ready for the exam itself. You must do some preliminary research on the test. Consult, for instance, the "sample test questions" book. The SAT, ACT, GRE, LSAT, and others have preparation books with information about their specific exam. We provide you with some of this information in Chapter 9.

Here are some questions whose answers you must research:

1. Is there a penalty for guessing? Know the scoring plan.

2. Do the same directions apply to all parts of the test?

3. Can you answer the questions in any order you wish?

4. Can you return to earlier incomplete sections?

Below are some points to remember when taking the exam:

1. Recording the answer in the wrong place may happen to you if you are not careful. A teacher with twelve years' experience of telling his students to carefully read the test instructions before taking the test told us that he recently took a standardized test and marked his answers on the score sheet *down* rather than properly *across*. This mistake can happen to anyone in the heat of battle. Don't let it happen to you. Be aware of the scoring procedure.

2. Don't jump to hasty conclusions. You must develop the habit of working carefully, but at a rapid pace, and of suspending your final judgment until you are sure you have done all you can to find the correct answer. In

mathematics, don't stop short of the final process. A selection may be partly correct but wrong, so read the choices completely.

3. Think through answers about which you are not certain. A shrewd inference is a form of educated guess which may produce the correct answer. An inference is based on partial knowledge and good reasoning. Although not a sure method, it is a workable one worth using on selected problems.

4. When you take an exam, resolve to work at top efficiency the whole time.

5. Misreading directions can be costly. Some sections call for least/most, smallest/ largest, true/false, or some other distinction. Students often answer with the "most" choice when the directions call for the "least" choice. Circling the key word may help you to avoid this unfortunate mistake.

6. If the questions are the objectively scored types, go straight through and answer all that you can answer easily first. Then return to work on the difficult ones.

7. Read the whole question carefully. Know exactly what the test maker wants you to do. Test takers often read into the question an inference not really there.

8. Do not hurry through the test. Test takers sometimes panic at the length of a test and feel they must rush through to complete it on time. It is easy to make a wrong interpretation of an item or to make some other mistake under these circumstances. Many standardized tests penalize for wrong answers, so accuracy can be most important, not speed.

9. Keeping your score sheet neat is a small but important factor. Erase small marks

mistakenly put on the score sheet. Do not let marks stray outside the appropriate spaces. Remember, the scoring machine does not recognize obvious mistakes, only the marks which appear on the sheet.

10. Confusing answer symbols can cause you to lose valuable points. When selecting your answer, you may put down D instead of your true choice B. Be aware that your eyes may pick up C at the end of line-item B, and you may put down the wrong letter mark because it was the last one you saw and it registered in your mind when you made your mark.

11. Faulty mathematical computations can cost you a good score. Double check your calculations, especially the simple ones— addition, subtraction, etc. Confusing units of measurement is a common mistake. Going through the correct steps and coming up with the wrong answer is a recurring error.

12. Be one of the last to hand in your score sheet. Use any extra time to check your answers. Test takers often find many careless mistakes when going over the test a second or third time.

13. Avoid postmortems. Your friends' answers may differ from yours and you may assume, perhaps mistakenly, that your answers are wrong. Don't cause yourself to worry by talking about the test items before you know your score.

We have suggested many "do's" and "don't's" of test taking. Our purpose was not to "straight-jacket" your life just before an exam, but to get you to think about what you are doing. Now, can you add to our pointers?

PART III

TESTS AND
TEST SCORES

CHAPTER 8

Your Test Results and Interpretation

The purpose of your taking tests is to help make decisions about you. Some decisions will be made by you. Some will be made by others. All of these decisions will be based on the interpretation of the results of your tests.

What kinds of decisions will be made? Generally there are three types of decisions made on the basis of test results:

1. There are decisions regarding your admission into various programs or institutions (this includes scholarships). You will be either accepted or rejected.

2. There are decisions regarding your placement within various programs or institutions. You may be classified for this or that group, level, or treatment.

3. There are evaluation decisions regarding your achievement or ability. You may be evaluated within some range (such as from high to low or from competent to incompetent). Decisions of this type often underlie the preceding types.

In order to help make such decisions, tests must yield results which have meaning or significance. That is, the results must be in some interpretable form.

In this chapter we will present some of the most common forms for reporting test results and some of the interpretation possibilities for these results. Your understanding of these ideas will help you to make decisions on the basis of your test performance. You will also have more understanding of the decisions made by others such as teachers and college admissions officials concerning your test performance. Such skill and understanding are needed to round out your development as a Master Test Taker.

TEACHER-MADE TEST RESULTS

The results of your tests will be reported to you in a summary form. For teacher-made tests the summary form of your results is usually one of (or a combination of) the following: raw scores, percentage scores, or letter grades.

Raw scores are numerical summaries of test performance. Your raw score may be the sum of your correct responses or the number of points assigned, as on an essay exam.

Percentage scores are also numerical reports of test performance. A percentage score is calculated by dividing the number of possible points into the number of earned points. For example, if there are 50 possible points and your raw score is 40 points, your percentage score is:

$$50 \overline{\smash{)}\begin{array}{r} .80 \\ 40.00 \\ \underline{40\,0} \\ 00 \end{array}} \qquad \text{or } 80\%.$$

Raw scores and percentage scores have little or no meaning to you until they are converted to letter grades or marks.

Letter grades or marks have attached meaning or significance even though not always clearly stated. For illustration, we will use the familiar A, B, C, D, and F form of letter-grade scale. These letters are commonly related to descriptive words which have meaning to us, such as: A = excellent, B = good, C = average, D = poor, and F = failure. Some teachers use a more elaborate specification in terms of goal achievement and the future:

A   All important and less important goals have been achieved, and the achievement is considerably above the minimum level required for doing more advanced work in the same subject.

B   All important goals have been achieved, but you have failed to achieve some of the less important goals. You have, however, achieved to the point where the goals of work at the next level could be attained by you.

C   All important goals have been achieved, but many of the less important goals have not been achieved. You have the minimum amount of preparation necessary for taking more advanced work in the same subject.

D   A few of the important goals may have been achieved, but your achievement is so limited that you are not well prepared to work at a more advanced level in the same subject.

F   None of the important goals have been achieved. Continuation in this subject cannot be recommended on the basis of this performance.

It should be mentioned that the above

scheme is only one of many that could be developed. The meanings of the letter grades necessarily reflect the educational philosophy upon which they are based.

If the summary form of your test results is simply a letter grade, you may make interpretations according to the criteria in the scheme above or according to some other scheme. Your school may have an officially adopted interpretation, or your teacher may have a scheme that reflects his or her educational philosophy. Of course many students develop their own meanings for various letter grades or marks.

If your results are in the form of a raw score or percentage score, then a translation scale is needed to locate yourself within a letter grade. Such conversion scales are often provided by teachers or administrators. For example, suppose your percentage score is 80 percent correct. Find your letter grade on this test.

Percent Correct	Letter Grade
90-100	A
80-89	B
70-79	C
60-69	D
0-59	F

Now it is possible to interpret your percentage score in a more meaningful way.

So far we have discussed the interpretation of your test results based on some specified criteria, the meanings attached to letter grades. It is also possible to interpret your score in terms of your standing relative to others who took the same test. To do this you would need information about how the others performed. For example, the teacher may present a tally of how many people achieved each letter grade. By locating yourself in such a tally you can get some idea of your performance compared to others. Raw scores can be treated mathematically so as to yield certain statistics such as the *average* (the sum of all scores divided by the number of scores) the *median* (the middle score when the scores are rank ordered), and the *mode* (the score which occurs most often). You can compare your raw score with these measures of the central tendency of the entire group. For example, you may conclude, "My score is 20 points above average," or, "My score falls just below the median of the class," or, "My score was above the mode for the class."

Raw scores, percentage scores, and letter grades can easily be misinterpreted. First, since these summary forms depend on the difficulty of the items on a test, it is not possible to compare directly the results of your scores or grades on different tests of the same subject. A score of 70 percent on one test might represent a level of ability which would be equal to only 30 percent on a more difficult test. Without some way of reliably comparing the difficulty of the two tests, you are left estimating or guessing.

Second, differences in raw scores or percentages or letter grades do not represent true differences in ability between individuals. Suppose, on a history test, Tom gets 42 points, Dick gets 45 points, and Harry gets 48 points. The raw score differences are equal. But is Tom truly as different from Dick as Dick is from Harry? There is no way to be sure because the raw scores depend upon which test items are being used. On a different exam testing the same ability they may change in relationship to each other. Perhaps Tom actually has more knowledge in history but the teacher did not use items which tested Tom's knowledge uniformly. Harry was lucky. He studied just the things which happened to be covered by the test. He knows little else.

Third, we cannot interpret test scores as we do some physical measures. For example, length has a true zero point (the absence of length) and equal units along the scale. This allows us to say, for instance, that one person is twice as tall as another, or has attained 50 percent of his probable adult height. We cannot make statements like this about test results. Suppose you scored 40 percent in vocabulary. Would this mean that you know only 40 percent of the words you should? No, for the teacher probably did not ask about easy words that you were sure to know. Even if you scored zero on the test it would not mean zero ability in vocabulary. The difference between you with a score of 40 percent, and the model student who earns 100 percent, is perhaps a difference in ability to define only 30 words out of a vocabulary of several thousand, assuming that those 30 constituted the test. A raw score of 60 in math may appear to represent ability twice as great as a raw score of 30, but the test probably does not include the problems everyone can solve. If people were tested on every possible type of math problem, the true ratio between them might be 1030 to 1060, or 10,030 to 10,060. True zero in ability is the complete absence of ability.

CHAPTER 9

Test Information

Our purpose in this chapter is to present general information on selected company-made standardized tests. The tests covered are High School Equivalency Examination (General Educational Development or GED), Preliminary Scholastic Aptitude Test (PSAT), Scholastic Aptitude Test (SAT), American College Testing Program (ACT), Graduate Record Examination (GRE), Graduate Management Admission Test (GMAT), and Law School Admission Test (LSAT). These exams are representative of three levels of educational testing: secondary school completion, college entrance, and graduate or professional entrance examinations. Owing to space limitations, many other types of exams (for example, civil service, medical, dental) have not been included.

Because high school completion requirements are controlled by state governments, registration requirements and issuance of diplomas or certificates vary from state to state. Minimum state age requirements for taking the GED range from 18 to 21 years. Some states, on the other hand, do not recognize the GED test at all.

All three test levels share basic test similarities, but differ in difficulty. Some tests have separate sections to test specific abilities 127 or knowledge (for instance, GRE tests a student's knowledge of his chosen field through an Advanced Test). But they all have verbal and mathematical sections.

The verbal section is divided into two categories (although the GRE adds to these a section on analytical abilities).

1. Correct use of English (grammar and usage).

2. Reading ability (comprehension, interpretation, and vocabulary).

The mathematics section calls for a familiarity with no more than two years high school equivalency (algebra and plane geometry). These tests challenge your developed abilities, not your specific knowledge.

In general no specific preparation will help you on the verbal and math sections. These tests aim to discover abilities developed over a period of years. But on specific sections (such as the GRE Advanced Test), it would help to review either your notes from college courses in your subject area or to read a good survey textbook in your subject area.

Do not guess on test items unless you can eliminate more than two or three choices. The one exception is the ACT, where you are told to complete all items and guess on the ones you do not know. All the other exams penalize you ¼ point per wrong answer. You are not penalized, however, for not answering test items.

All testing services claim their examinations are highly reliable. They quote statistics and point out the company's long experience in the field as proof of their exam's reliability.

They all underscore the fact that their examination is only one consideration used by colleges to determine entrance to higher education.

If you need materials or information on a test, here are the addresses and phone numbers of the above mentioned examinations:

ACT: ACT Registration
      P.O. Box 414
      Iowa City, IA 52240
      Phone: (319) 356-3794

SAT: College Board ATP
      Box 592
      Princeton, NJ 08541
      Phone: (609) 921-9000

PSAT: PSAT/NMSQT
      Box 589
      Princeton, NJ 08541
      Phone: (609) 921-9000

      (Southwest and Western States)
      Box 1025
      Berkeley, CA 94701
      Phone: (415) 849-0950

GRE: Graduate Record Examination
      Box 955
      Princeton, NJ 08541
      Phone: (609) 921-9000

GMAT: GMAT
      Educational Testing Service
      Box 966
      Princeton, NJ 08541
      Phone: (609) 921-9000

LSAT: Law School Admissions Services
Box 944
Princeton, NJ 08541
Phone: (609) 921-9000

For the GED test, call your local school district office for the address to write to for materials and information.

CHAPTER 10

Readiness Checklist

How do you know when you are prepared to take a test? In the final analysis, you are the one who must decide whether or not you are ready. Below is a checklist to help you determine your preparedness. If you can answer yes to the following questions, you may consider yourself ready for your test.

1. Do I know the pitfalls of being improperly prepared when arriving at the test site and while taking the test?

2. Do I know the purpose of the examination?

3. Have I done all I can to investigate the nature of the test?

4. Do I know the scope of the examination?

5. Have I practiced good health habits?

6. Do I know the date and place of the test?

7. Have I reviewed properly for the test (for a teacher-made exam, it is the assignments; for a company-made exam, it is a sample test items review book)?

8. Do I know which subjects will be tested?

9. Have I scheduled my time so as to be adequately prepared?

10. Do I know the total time allowed for each test section?

11. Have I learned to overcome test anxiety? 131

12. Do I know the forms of the questions (objectively scored items and/or essay items)?

13. Do I know the equipment needed and allowed at the testing site?

14. Have I made a commitment to myself to practice good study habits?

15. Have I overcome negative attitudes and determined to practice positive attitudes toward test taking?

16. Can I use the memory techniques presented in chapter 6 for test preparation (if applicable)?

17. Do I know the total time allowed for the examination?

18. Have I achieved test-taking confidence?

With this book, you can totally prepare yourself for tests. You are not assured, however, of higher scores than you actually merit. You are assured of an opportunity to score as high as you deserve on tests. You may achieve this aim, we believe, when you successfully attain the goals set forth for you in this book.

Appendix

Answers to Study Habits/Test-Taking Skills Appraisal

A. General Habits and Methods of Study

12. F	37. F	45. F	55. F
13. F	38. T	46. F	
14. T	39. T	47. T	
15. F	40. F	48. F	
16. T	41. F	49. F	
17. F	42. T	50. T	
18. F	43. T	51. T	
19. T	44. F	53. F	

B. Habits and Techniques of Reading

4. F	28. F	34. F
5. F	29. F	56. T
7. T	30. T	60. T
11. T	32. T	

C. Attitudes toward School

27. F	57. T
33. T	58. T
35. F	
36. F	

D. Taking Notes and Writing Papers

8. T	22. F	25. T	52. F
10. F	23. T	26. F	
20. T	24. F	31. T	

E. Preparing for and Taking Tests

1. F	9. F	59. F
2. F	21. F	
3. T	54. F	
6. T